OCS Report MMS 2005-011

Linking Water Turbidity and Total Suspended Solids Loading to Kelp Productivity within the Stefansson Sound Boulder Patch
ANIMIDA Task 6 (Boulder Patch)

Final Report to
Minerals Management Service
Contract 1435-01-99-CT-30998, TO 10906

Ken Dunton, Adrian Burd, Dale Funk, and Robert Maffione, PI's
Report Prepared by Craig Aumack

March 2004

 **U.S. Department of the Interior**
Minerals Management Service
Alaska Outer Continental Shelf Region

The Department of the Interior Mission

As the Nation's principal conservation agency, the Department of the Interior has responsibility for most of our nationally owned public lands and natural resources. This includes fostering sound use of our land and water resources; protecting our fish, wildlife, and biological diversity; preserving the environmental and cultural values of our national parks and historical places; and providing for the enjoyment of life through outdoor recreation. The Department assesses our energy and mineral resources and works to ensure that their development is in the best interests of all our people by encouraging stewardship and citizen participation in their care. The Department also has a major responsibility for American Indian reservation communities and for people who live in island territories under U.S. administration.

The Minerals Management Service Mission

As a bureau of the Department of the Interior, the Minerals Management Service's (MMS) primary responsibilities are to manage the mineral resources located on the Nation's Outer Continental Shelf (OCS), collect revenue from the Federal OCS and onshore Federal and Indian lands, and distribute those revenues.

Moreover, in working to meet its responsibilities, the **Offshore Minerals Management Program** administers the OCS competitive leasing program and oversees the safe and environmentally sound exploration and production of our Nation's offshore natural gas, oil and other mineral resources. The MMS **Royalty Management Program** meets its responsibilities by ensuring the efficient, timely and accurate collection and disbursement of revenue from mineral leasing and production due to Indian tribes and allottees, States and the U.S. Treasury.

The MMS strives to fulfill its responsibilities through the general guiding principles of: (1) being responsive to the public's concerns and interests by maintaining a dialogue with all potentially affected parties and (2) carrying out its programs with an emphasis on working to enhance the quality of life for all Americans by lending MMS assistance and expertise to economic development and environmental protection.

LINKING WATER TURBIDITY AND TOTAL SUSPENDED SOLIDS LOADING TO KELP PRODUCTIVITY WITHIN THE STEFANSSON SOUND BOULDER PATCH

ANIMIDA Task 6 (Boulder Patch)

March 2003

Ken Dunton[1], Adrian Burd[2], Dale Funk[3], and Robert Maffione[4], PI's
Report Prepared by Craig Aumack[1]

[1]The University of Texas Marine Science Institute, 750 Channel View Drive, Port Aransas, TX 78373
(361) 749-6728, FAX (361) 749-6777, E-mail: dunton@utmsi.utexas.edu;

[2]Department of Marine Science, University of Georgia, Athens, GA 30602-3636
(706) 542-1604, FAX (704) 542-5888, E-mail: adrianb@arches.uga.edu;

[3]LGL Alaska Research Associates, Inc. 1101 East 76th Ave. Suite B, Anchorage, AK 99518
(907) 562-3339; FAX (907) 562-7223; E-mail: dfunk@lgl.com

[4]HOBI-Laboratories, 8987 E. Tanque Verde #309-366, Tucson, AZ 85749
(520) 299-2598, FAX (520) 299-2598, E-mail: maffione@hobilabs.com;

This study was funded by the U.S. Department of the Interior, Minerals Management Service (MMS), Alaska Outer Continental Shelf Region, Anchorage Alaska, under Contract No. 1435-01-99-CT-30998, TO 10906, as part of the MMS Alaska Environmental Studies Program.

The opinions, findings, conclusions, or recommendations expressed in this report or product are those of the authors and do not necessarily reflect the views of the U.S. Department of the Interior, nor does mention of trade names or commercial products constitute endorsement or recommendation for use by the Federal Government.

Project Organization Page

Responsibilities	IOP Collection	TSS	Chl *a*	Nutrients	Physiochemical Data	Kelp Growth
Field Collection	Ken Dunton, Craig Aumack, Dale Funk, Robert Maffione	Ken Dunton, Craig Aumack, Dale Funk	Ken Dunton, Craig Aumack, Dale Funk	Ken Dunton, Craig Aumack, Dale Funk	Ken Dunton, Craig Aumack, Dale Funk, Robert Maffione	Ken Dunton, Craig Aumack
Laboratory Analyses	--	Craig Aumack, Dale Funk, Ken Dunton	Craig Aumack	Craig Aumack	--	Craig Aumack, Dale Funk, Ken Dunton
Data Entry	Craig Aumack	Craig Aumack	Craig Aumack	Craig Aumack	Craig Aumack	Craig Aumack
Model Design and Analysis	Adrian Burd, Robert Maffione, Craig Aumack	Adrian Burd, Robert Maffione, Craig Aumack	--	--	--	--
Statistics	Craig Aumack	Craig Aumack	Craig Aumack	Craig Aumack	--	Craig Aumack
Report Generation	Ken Dunton, Craig Aumack, Dale Funk, Adrian Burd	Ken Dunton, Craig Aumack, Dale Funk, Adrian Burd	Ken Dunton, Craig Aumack, Dale Funk, Adrian Burd	Ken Dunton, Craig Aumack, Dale Funk, Adrian Burd	Ken Dunton, Craig Aumack, Dale Funk, Adrian Burd	Ken Dunton, Craig Aumack, Dale Funk, Adrian Burd

Table of Contents

Executive Summary

The Stefansson Sound Boulder Patch, located 20 km northeast of Prudhoe Bay in the Alaskan Beaufort Sea, supports the only known kelp bed on the Alaskan arctic coast that is characterized by high benthic diversity associated with an abundance of boulders, cobbles, and pebbles. Growth and production of the endemic arctic kelp *Laminaria solidungula*, which is abundant throughout the area, is regulated primarily by PAR (photosynthetically active radiation) availability during the summer open-water period. Variation in underwater PAR, caused by changes in water transparency, can have significant effects on the annual productivity of this species (Dunton, 1990). Although the physiological responses of *L. solidungula* to changes in PAR are well described, the relationship between PAR and water turbidity (measured in terms of total suspended solids [TSS]) is poorly understood. Consequently, our ability to assess the effects of changes in water transparency, whether caused by natural or anthropogenic events, is significantly compromised.

In an attempt to further our understanding of the relationship between TSS and light availability, we measured the inherent optical properties (IOPs) of Stefansson Sound waters, including absorption, scattering, and attenuation, in conjunction with TSS concentrations for a two-week period in summers 2001 and 2002. These data were used in a radiative transfer equation (RTE), and a TSS concentration specific attenuation coefficient [$K^*_d(\lambda,H)$] was determined. The attenuation coefficient was inserted into a productivity model to estimate daily kelp production throughout the Boulder Patch. Our model output agreed well with previously published measurements of annual kelp production based on the number of hours of saturating irradiance available to the kelp under average water transparency conditions.

1

The highest TSS levels ($23.0 - 24.2$ mg L^{-1}) occurred in nearshore areas during summer 2001 and were coincident with increased light attenuation ($11.4 - 14.0$ m^{-1}). In both years, lower TSS concentrations and lower light attenuations were measured in areas furthest from the coast within the Boulder Patch kelp community. Although light attenuation through the water column decreased in summer 2002, attenuation and TSS were significantly correlated ($p < 0.01$).

Our results clearly demonstrate that suspended sediment concentrations have varying but substantial affects on light availability, and subsequent kelp production, during the summer open-water period. Increasing average TSS concentrations from 1 to 10 mg L^{-1}, within ranges measured *in situ*, decreased annual production by an order of magnitude. Even under an array of surface irradiance budgets, production estimates and rates changed substantially under different TSS concentrations. Production, modeled under a variety of summer surface light regimes, was always higher at lower TSS concentrations and estimated kelp production was higher in offshore locations, despite deeper depths, because they are characterized by lower TSS.

The accuracy of the model was tested using previously recorded surface irradiance data from 1990 and 1991. In both years, model estimated production coincided well with annual production calculated from blade length data. Similar accuracy was demonstrated when the model was used to estimate annual production for 2001. Although previous years' estimates coincided with those calculated using blade length data, estimates for 2002 production were distinctly different. This was most likely the result of temporal sampling bias. Low TSS concentrations recorded during a two-week period in summer 2002 were probably not representative of water conditions for the entire summer open water season in 2002. Consequently, reasonable estimates of kelp production using this model are dependent on TSS, IOP, and surface light measurements reflective of overall summer conditions.

Introduction

Unconsolidated sediments composed of silty clays and mud generally characterize the nearshore Alaskan Beaufort Sea, but areas of hard rock substratum also occur along portions of the coast (Dunton *et al.*, 1982). In Stefansson Sound, these deposits are incorporated into the Gubik formation and support abundant kelp and diverse epilithic fauna. The boulders, cobbles, and pebbles contain mineral types that are clearly extrinsic to northern Alaska (MacCarthy, 1958; Hopkins, 1979; Dunton *et al.*, 1982) and suggest that rocks were transported from arctic Canada during the last glaciation (MacCarthy, 1958; Hopkins, 1979). These rocks provide a solid substratum needed for kelp colonization (Dunton *et al.*, 1982; Busdosh *et al.*, 1985). Consequently, kelp beds occupy areas of rocky substratum within Stefansson Sound and support a diverse community of kelp and epilithic invertebrates collectively known as the Boulder Patch.

Similar to other kelp dominated ecosystems, sunlight, nutrient availability, and temperature are important abiotic factors regulating primary production. Among these, light displays the largest variation. In polar regions, solar irradiance changes dramatically with season (Lüning and Dring, 1979; Chapman and Lindley, 1980; Dunton, 1990; Kirst and Wiencke, 1995) and at 70° N, annual solar radiation is 30 to 50% less than temperate and equatorial regions (Kondratyev, 1954). The Arctic's already restricted light availability is compounded in the Boulder Patch by formation of 2-m thick fast ice in the nearshore Beaufort Sea during the long seven-month winter season. These factors contribute to poor light availability for kelp growing within Stefansson Sound.

Marine flora have a variety of adaptive responses that help compensate for lower irradiances at high latitudes. For example, the endemic arctic kelp *Laminaria solidungula* completes over 90% of its annual linear growth during the dark nine-month ice covered winter period (Dunton and Schell, 1986). Kelp utilize carbon reserves accumulated during the previous summer when waters are predominantly free of ice and light is available (Chapman and Lindley, 1980; Hooper, 1984; Dunton, 1985; Dunton and Schell, 1986; Henley and Dunton, 1995). Photosynthetic production during the open-water period is usually sufficient to compensate for respiratory demands and allow accumulation of carbon storage compounds. However, large variations in underwater irradiance can occur during summer depending on sediment concentrations in the water column. Suspended sediments decrease water transparency and may significantly reduce annual kelp productivity (Dunton, 1990; Best *et al.*, 2001).

Research studies have clearly documented that growth and productivity of kelp within Stefansson Sound are regulated by light availability (photosynthetically active radiation [PAR]) during the summer open-water season (Henley and Dunton, 1997). Results from a variety of experimental studies, including the linear growth response of kelp to natural changes in the underwater light field (Dunton, 1984; Dunton and Schell, 1986; Dunton, 1990), carbon radioisotope tracer experiments (Dunton and Jodwalis, 1988), and laboratory and field physiological work (Henley and Dunton, 1995; 1997), have been used successfully to develop models relating kelp productivity to PAR.

However, PAR availability in the summer open-water period is not constant and is largely a function of water transparency, measured by the amount of total suspended solids (TSS; Table 1) in the local area (Henley and Dunton, 1995). TSS are particles in the water column that diminish sub-surface irradiance. These particles include clay, silt, sand, decaying vegetation and animals, or any inanimate particulate matter (Kirk, 1983). TSS originates from erosion, industrial or natural discharge, run-off, dredging, and flocculation. As these suspended particulates move through the water column, they reflect, refract, and absorb sunlight, thereby reducing light availability for macroalgal photosynthesis and biomass production. Ultimately, reduced kelp production means less food and habitat for organisms dependent on the kelp forest.

Spatial and temporal TSS variations alter the number of hours kelp are exposed to levels of saturating irradiance (H_{sat}). H_{sat} for *Laminaria solidungula* in the Boulder Patch has ranged from as low as 39 hours to as high as 171 hours in a single summer (Dunton, 1990). Despite known variations in irradiance levels reaching the kelp canopy during summer and the impact of reduced summer light on annual kelp production, the relationship between TSS and PAR is poorly understood. Consequently, it has been difficult, if not impossible, to accurately estimate productivity on the basis of TSS data alone.

TSS concentrations should be linearly related to light attenuation by particles in the water column (Di Toro, 1978; Kirk, 1984b; Van Duin *et al.*, 2001; Maffione *et al.*, 2003). Attenuation (k), or the fraction of radiant energy removed from light per unit distance through a given media, is quantified by two important optical parameters, absorption and scattering (Van De Hulst, 1957; Kirk, 1983; 1984a; 1984b; Maffione, 1998; Van Duin *et al.*, 2001). Absorption (a) occurs when photons are absorbed throughout the water column by colored dissolved organic matter (CDOM), biological organisms, suspended sediment, and the water itself (Kirk, 1983; Van Duin *et al.*, 2001). Scattering (b) does not remove a significant fraction of photons but increases the effective length of photon travel, thereby increasing the probability of being absorbed (Kirk, 1983; Van Duin *et al.*, 2001). High ratios of scattering coefficient to absorption coefficient ($b{:}a$) are typically affiliated with areas of increased turbidities (Kirk, 1994). Coastal regions receiving high river discharge or shallow waters with unconsolidated sediments often have high $b{:}a$ ratios (> 30), a direct result of increased TSS, which are typically correlated with photon scattering rather than absorption (Van

6

De Hulst, 1957). Connections between PAR and TSS concentrations in Stefansson Sound can be quantified through measurement of these two inherent optical properties (IOPs). Once determined, the IOPs in Stefansson Sound can be used to develop attenuation coefficients for PAR penetration to the seabed. With this information, we can determine potential changes in primary production in response to varying water transparency, caused by changes in TSS concentration, throughout Stefansson Sound.

The objective of this study was to determine the influence of suspended sediments during the summer season on the productivity of *Laminaria solidungula* in Stefansson Sound. We did this by quantifying the inherent optical properties and their relationship to suspended particulates in the water column. Once accomplished, we developed an attenuation coefficient based on specific TSS concentrations $[K^{*}_{d}(\lambda,H)]$. This coefficient allowed us to estimate benthic irradiance levels based on surface PAR measurements and water depth. Published photosynthesis versus irradiance curves were used in conjunction with calculated benthic irradiance levels to attain a reasonable production estimate for the coming growth year (GWYR). Proximity of the Sagavanirktok River Delta outflow, along with the shallow depths, silty bottoms, and high turbidities that characterize Stefansson Sound indicate that light attenuation should be heavily influenced by suspended sediment concentrations. Kelp production, directly related to summer irradiance, will be indirectly impacted by TSS concentrations. We hypothesize that kelp beds located further offshore should be characterized by relatively higher rates of annual productivity, despite the deeper depths, because lower concentrations of TSS permit significantly higher light penetration to the seabed.

Materials and Methods

Study Area

    This study was conducted within Stefansson Sound (70°25' N; 147°80' W), which lies 20 km northeast of Prudhoe Bay in the Alaskan Beaufort Sea (Figure 1). Stefansson Sound extends from the Midway Islands in the west to Tigvariak Island in the east and is enclosed by a barrier island chain to the north. Holocene marine deposits of silts and mud generally characterize the Stefansson Sound seabed, boulders and cobbles cover various areas. These areas of solid benthos are collectively referred to as the Stefansson Sound Boulder Patch. The Boulder Patch covers over 20 km^2 (Dunton, 1984) and provides the substratum necessary for a diverse assemblage of invertebrates and macroalgae. The most dominant organism is the kelp *Laminaria solidungula*, which constitutes over 90% of phaeophyte biomass in the Boulder Patch (Dunton *et al.*, 1982).

    Fieldwork for this study was conducted from Endicott Island, a British Petroleum Exploration (Alaska) owned and operated facility near the mouth of the Sagavanirktok River Delta during summers 2001 through 2003. Samples and measurements were obtained in the field using the R/V Proteus, a 7.6 m (25 foot) Boston Whaler equipped for arctic coastal work. Terminology and units for parameters measured or calculated as part of this study are listed in Table 1.

    The National Climatic Data Center (www.ncdc.noaa.gov), using a 30-yr record, characterized the following average summer weather conditions along the North Slope; temperature (39.6°C), wind speed (19.3 km hr^{-1}), and cloud cover (70.5 d summer^{-1}). Based on personal observations from Stefansson Sound, weather patterns are difficult to predict and changes are periodic and sudden. Wind speed, precipitation, and sea surface conditions are all highly variable and dependent on changing wind directions (NW, E, SE, SW).

Light Measurements

In situ water column absorbance and attenuation were measured using an ac-9 (WET Labs Inc., Philomath, Oregon, USA), which simultaneously determines the spectral transmittance and spectral absorbance over nine wavelengths (412, 440, 488, 510, 532, 555, 630, 676, and 715 nm) and calculates the absorption (a) and attenuation (k) of the water at those frequencies (www.wetlabs.com). The instrument was towed at a constant speed, $4.0 - 6.5$ km hr^{-1}, behind the R/V Proteus at 0.10 and 0.50 m. depths. Measurements were made along predetermined transects in and around Stefansson Sound and the Boulder Patch during summers 2001 and 2002 (Figure 2). Daily tracklines included transects both inside and outside the Boulder Patch for comparison. Most transects outside the Boulder Patch were in coastal waters between the Boulder Patch and shoreline. Measurements were downloaded, averaged over 1-min intervals, and corrected by subtracting the specific wavelength's pure water correction value. Once completed, absorption was scatter-corrected (www.wetlabs.com) and matched to its congruent geographic location. Similarly, the ac-9 was used to conduct vertical profiles at 11 different locations (Figure 3). Profiles at routine sampling locations were taken at different times of the day to examine diel changes in light transmittance.

PAR was measured continuously at DS-11 from 28 July to 8 August 2002. DS-11, the site of highest kelp biomass, was chosen because of its historical relevance. Data were collected using four underwater light sensors, two LI-193SA spherical quantum sensors and two LI-190SA underwater cosine sensors, connected to two LI-1000 dataloggers (LI-COR Inc., Lincoln, Nebraska, USA). Sensors were mounted on PVC poles and positioned just above the kelp canopy to prevent fouling or shading by kelp fronds. Instantaneous PAR measurements were taken at 1-min intervals and integrated over 1-hr periods. Subsequent surface PAR measurements were taken with two LI-190SA terrestrial cosine sensors connected to two LI-1000 dataloggers located at nearby Endicott Island. Sensors were placed on the roofs of two stationary storage containers to eliminate shading. Data from both sets of paired dataloggers were graphed and compared statistically to ensure similar results.

Total Suspended Solids (TSS)

To determine *in situ* TSS during summers 2001 and 2002, three replicate water samples were sampled at collection sites along transects and at several depths during vertical profiles (Figure 4). Water was forced to the surface through plastic tubing from the ac-9's internal water pump and collected on the surface in 1-L plastic bottles. Bottles were labeled and sampling point geographic coordinates (Lat/Long) recorded using a handheld Garmin Global Positioning System, GPSMap 76S (Garmin International Inc., Olathe, Kansas, USA). Samples were stored in a cooler and transported to a lab on Endicott Island for processing.

A known volume of water from each sample was filtered through pre-weighed, pre-combusted 4-mm glass fiber filters (Pall Corporation, Ann Arbor, Michigan, USA). Filters were oven dried to constant weight at 65°C. The net weight of particles collected in each sample was calculated by subtracting the filter's initial weight from the total weight following filtration. Weights were determined with a microbalance (Denver Instruments APX-60, Arvada, Colorado, USA).

Chlorophyll Concentrations

At each collection site (Figure 4), water for chlorophyll measurements was sampled in triplicate using 1-L plastic bottles. Water was collected from depths

(0 – 8 m) using the ac-9. Bottles were stored in a dark cooler and transported to Endicott Island. In the dark, 100 ml of water from each replicate sample was filtered through a 0.45 μm cellulose nitrate membrane filter (Whatman, Maidstone, England). After filtration, the filters and residue were placed in pre-labeled 10 ml Crio-Vials and frozen in liquid nitrogen. The frozen filters were transported to The University of Texas Marine Science Institute (UTMSI) in Port Aransas, Texas for subsequent chlorophyll analysis.

At UTMSI, filters were removed from the vials and placed in pre-labeled test tubes containing 10 ml of methanol for overnight extraction (Parsons *et al.*, 1984). Chlorophyll *a* concentration, in μg L^{-1}, was determined using a Turner Designs 10-AU fluorometer (Turner Design, Sunnyvale, California, USA). Non-acidification techniques were used to account for the presence of chlorophyll b and phaeopigments (Welschmeyer, 1994).

Radiative Transfer Equation and Productivity Model

IOPs obtained in the field were used in a Radiative Transfer Equation (RTE; Maffione, 2003; Maffione *et al.*, 2003):

$$K_d(\lambda,H) = \frac{\ln[E_d(\lambda,0^+)/E_d(\lambda,H)]}{H} \quad (1.1)$$

where $K_d(\lambda,H)$ is the bulk downwelling irradiance attenuation coefficient at depth (H), $E_d(\lambda,0^+)$ denotes the downwelling spectral irradiance incident on the water's surface (0^+), and $E_d(\lambda,H)$ is the downwelling spectral irradiance incident at depth H. $K_d(\lambda,H)$ was computed for a range of TSS concentrations (C_{TSS}), and a linear regression of $K_d(\lambda,H)$ vs. C_{TSS} was performed. The slope of this regression denotes the sediment concentration specific attenuation coefficient $[K^*_d(\lambda,H)]$ (Van Duin *et al.*, 2001). Once $K^*_d(\lambda,H)$ was established, $E_d(\lambda,H)$ or the downwelling spectral irradiance incident at depth H, was easily computed for any TSS concentration:

$$E_d(\lambda,H) = E_d(\lambda,0^+) \exp[-K^*_d(\lambda,H) \cdot C_{TSS} \cdot H]. \qquad (1.2)$$

Accurate $K_d(\lambda,H)$ for Stefansson Sound is crucial for calculating reasonable productivity estimates. Since $K_d(\lambda,H)$ is a function of the relationship between the IOPs and TSS, annual comparisons between these two parameters were statistically verified prior to insertion into the RTE. Additionally, accuracy of the final $K_d(\lambda,H)$ was determined through *in situ* irradiance measurements taken in 2002 (refer to <u>Light Measurements</u> section). Input of the calculated $K^*_d(\lambda,H)$ into equation (1.2) along with known surface spectral irradiance $(E_d(\lambda,0^+))$, TSS concentration (C_{TSS}), and depth (H) yielded bottom irradiance measurements $(E_d(\lambda,H))$ comparable to *in situ* measurements.

Results from the RTE were coupled with a clear-sky irradiance model (Gregg and Carder, 1990). The model computes spectral irradiance as well as PAR at the surface and applies the resulting $K^*_d(\lambda,H)$ based on measured TSS concentrations from the local area. Irradiance reaching the kelp canopy is calculated based on the effects of $K^*_d(\lambda,H)$ on surface irradiance and depth.

The model was designed specifically for marine atmospheres and includes factors for oxygen concentration, ozone and water absorption, aerosols, and sea-surface reflectance (Burd, 2003). Meteorological data required for the irradiance model, including air temperature (°C), relative humidity (%), and wind speed (m s^{-1}), were taken from NOAA National Data Center for the airport at Deadhorse,

Alaska (70° 11'N, 148° 29'W). This data center was chosen for its proximity to Stefansson Sound.

Additional required parameters include atmospheric pressure, some relative degree of aerosol (1 for open-ocean to 10 for continental atmosphere) based on Junge distributions that have been fitted to the Navy Aerosol Model (Gregg and Carder, 1990), and total amount of water precipitate in a 1-cm^2 area in a vertical path from the top of the atmosphere to the surface (h).   Here, h was calculated using the expression (Butler, 1998):

$$h = \frac{P_0}{3 \cdot T_0} \tag{1.3}$$

where h is in millimeters, T_0 is the surface temperature in Kelvin, and P_0 is the surface water vapor partial pressure. P_0 must be calculated from the equation:

$$P_0 = (2.409 \times 10^{12}) \cdot R \cdot \theta^4 \cdot e^{-22.640} \tag{1.4}$$

where R is relative humidity and $\theta = 300/ T_0$ is inverse temperature.

Photosynthetic rates (hourly, diel, or annual) in response to changing irradiance and respiration rates for *Laminaria solidungula* were obtained from published literature (Dunton and Jodwalis, 1988). Although a variety of formulas exist for estimating photosynthetic production as a function of incident irradiance, the following equation was chosen for its simplicity (Jassby and Platt, 1976):

$$P = P_{max} \cdot \tan h \left(\frac{I}{I_k} \right) \tag{1.5}$$

where P is calculated production, P_{max} is maximum photosynthetic production sustained assuming no photoinhibition, I_k is saturation irradiance, and I is irradiance available to algae. Although equation (1.5) was first developed for phytoplankton, it is valid for kelp because photosynthetic response to changing light concentrations is similar for many protists. Only basal blade biomass was modeled, as this is where the bulk of photosynthetic production occurs during summer (Dunton and Jodwalis, 1988).

Several assumptions and caveats exist that need consideration prior to interpreting results. The base model uses clear-sky irradiance without cloud cover influence. Although an arbitrary reduction factor (≤ 1) was applied to simulate cloud cover and reduce atmospheric irradiance concentrations, the simulation cannot accurately mimic overhead cloud effects (Burd, 2003). Alternatively, specific hourly surface or bottom irradiances can be entered into the model to provide productivity estimates for explicit conditions. Another limitation of the model is its inability to account for photoinhibition, or reduced photosynthetic production at high irradiances. Entering data in the equation (Platt *et al.*, 1980):

$$P = P_s (1-e^{-a}) e^{-b} \qquad (1.6)$$

where $P_s = P_{max}$, $a = \alpha I/P_s$ and $b = \beta I/P_s$ represents the effects of photoinhibition. Here, α is the initial slope of photosynthetic production per unit irradiance and β is the slope of photosynthetic production per unit irradiance once any increase in irradiance causes a decline in photosynthetic yield. This revealed no evidence of photoinhibition in basal blades and little evidence in secondary blades. Thus, the difference between using equation (1.5) and equation (1.6), including photoinhibition, proved minimal ($\approx 2\%$; Burd, 2003). This test was conducted with published data (Dunton and Jodwalis, 1988), and the results could vary between years. Model results were all calculated using Matlab 6.1 (The Mathworks Inc., Natick, Massachusetts, USA).

Model reasonability was determined through various artificial simulations throughout Stefansson Sound. At each of the 11 sampling sites, the model was used to generate daily production, in g C gdw^{-1} d^{-1}, based on a 60-d summer period and three fixed TSS concentrations (1, 10 , and 20 mg L^{-1}). Surface irradiance for any production estimate was model-generated and remained constant for all tests at all sites. Between fixed TSS concentrations, any difference in production could only be attributed to a change in site depth. Similarly, production differences between specific sites could only be attributed to varying TSS concentrations. These artificial production values were used to check model accuracy and determine potential effects of varying TSS concentrations on kelp production.

The influence of TSS on kelp production was examined over a range of insolation values to simulate changes in cloud cover based on *in situ* light measurements recorded in 1990 and 1991 by Dunton *et al.* Hourly irradiance values in 1990 and 1991 were increased or reduced by 10, 20, 30, 40, and 50% to create a variety of summer light conditions. Steady increments of TSS (1, 3, 5, 7, 9, 11, and 13 mg L^{-1}) were entered into the model under each of the light budgets. Productivity was then calculated throughout the summer season for all light budgets at each turbidity level. These were compared to determine the TSS influence on annual production under a variety of seasonal light levels. Subsequently, production percent increase over common ranges of increasing light levels (50 – 60%, 75 – 85%, 115 – 120%, and 140 – 150% incident irradiance for summers 1990 and 1991) was examined under three different TSS concentrations (1, 7, and 13 mg L^{-1}). Comparison allowed us to examine the

15

influence of TSS on set irradiance increases (10%) at various magnitudes of light in terms of production percentage.

Annual production estimates, in g C m^{-2} yr^{-1}, were calculated for each of the 11 sites for both 2001 and 2002. This was accomplished using TSS and IOP data measured *in situ* during their respective years. Modeled surface irradiance along with average annual site specific TSS concentrations were used as input to the production model. Estimated production, g C gdw^{-1} d^{-1}, was then extrapolated to a 60-d summer growth period. Based on previous calculations, assumed biomass of 39.3 gdw m^{-2} for boulder cover 25% or greater and 10.0 gdw m^{-2} for boulder cover between 10-25% were used to convert production units to g C m^{-2} yr^{-1} (Dunton et al., 1982).

Nutrient Concentrations

At six water collection sites (W-1, W-3, DS-11, E-1, Brower-1, and Narwhal Island), water for nutrient measurements was sampled in triplicate using 100 ml plastic bottles during summer 2002 (Figure 3). Water was collected from 2-m depth using the ac-9. At the offshore site, Narwhal Island, water samples for nutrients were collected at 2 and 8 m depth for comparison. Bottles were stored in a dark cooler and transported to Endicott Island where they were frozen. Water samples were then transferred to UTMSI for nutrient analysis. Nutrient concentrations (μM) for NH_4^+, $NO_2^- + NO_3^-$, and PO_4^{3-} were determined by continuous flow injection analysis using colorimetric techniques described in QuikChem Methods manual on a Lachat QuikChem 8000 (Zellweger Analytics Inc., Milwaukee, Wisconsin, USA) with a minimum detection level of 0.03 μM.

Physiochemical Parameters

Salinity (psu), depth (m), temperature (^{o}C), and water density (kg m^{-3}) were measured using a Seabird 911*plus* CTD (Sea-Bird Electronics Inc.,

Bellevue, Washington, USA). The instrument was towed behind the R/V Proteus at a constant speed (4.0 – 6.5 km hr^{-1}) along predetermined transects throughout Stefansson Sound (Figure 2). Depths ranged between 0.14 - 0.50 m. Measurements were recorded every 0.5 seconds. Data were imported to Microsoft Excel and averaged over 1-minute intervals. Mean values were assigned to their known geographic coordinates and interpolated across Stefansson Sound.

The CTD was also used to conduct vertical profiles in both 2001 and 2002. Vertical profiles were generally at 11-preset sampling stations throughout the Boulder Patch (Figure 3). These locations included seven dive sites (DS-11, E-1, E-2, E-3, L-1, L-2, Brower-1), three western sites (W-1, W-2, W-3), and one site located offshore near the barrier islands (Narwhal Island). Data were graphed and used to visually trace the vertical distribution of different water mass types.

Kelp Growth

At each of the seven dive sites within the Boulder Patch (DS-11, Brower-1, E-1, E-2, E-3, L-1, and L-2), SCUBA divers collected 15-30 individual specimens of *Laminaria solidungula* attached to large cobbles and boulders during summers 2001 through 2003 (Figure 3). Samples were placed in pre-labeled black bags, transported to Endicott, and processed. Blade lengths from every specimen, each corresponding to a different year's growth (Dunton, 1985), were measured and recorded to produce a recent (3-4 yr) growth record of linear expansion at each site. A growth year (GWYR) is defined as the period beginning 15 November one year and ending 15 November the following year.

Statistics and GIS

IOPs, final PAR measurements, TSS concentrations, chlorophyll *a* concentrations, and annual production estimates were matched with their respective geographic coordinates and plotted using GIS software ArcView 3.2 (ERSI, Redlands, California, 1999). ArcView 3.2 allowed point data collected in the field to be represented in a media aiding spatial contrast (Alexander and Dunton, 2002). Data were interpolated across a polygon of Stefansson Sound, including the Boulder Patch, using Spatial Analyst 3.0 extension and Inverse Distance Weighting function in ArcView 3.2. Using this technique, entered data acts as a reference point with a local influence that diminishes with distance. The interpolated values are more similar to data points closest to the respective value than those more distant.

All data were analyzed using standard parametric models. Spatial and inter-annual significance among IOP, TSS, and chlorophyll measurements were determined using a two-way analysis of variance (ANOVA) and Tukey multiple-comparison tests to examine significant differences ($p < 0.05$) among treatment variables using SPSS 10.0 (SPSS Inc., Chicago, Illinois, USA). Variation among measured light wavelengths was tested using a Principle Component Analysis (Primer-E Ltd, Plymouth Marine Laboratory, Plymouth, UK).

Results

Light Measurements

Distinct geographic differences in the IOPs occurred throughout Stefansson Sound in 2001 and 2002. Similar trends were noted at all quantified wavelengths. Furthermore, a principle component analysis indicated variance among measured wavelengths to be < 0.001. We chose to display coefficients collected at the 676 nm wavelength since this wavelength is most sensitive to changes in chlorophyll *a* (absorption peak is 670 nm) and TSS (Figures 5 – 10).

Absorption (*a*) coefficients ranged between $0.096 - 0.153$ m^{-1} and were highest along coastal zones between Endicott Island and Satellite Drilling Island (SDI), 0.153 and 0.144 m^{-1}, respectively, in 2001 (Figure 5). Increased *a* values were also present in offshore waters overlying the Boulder Patch, particularly in areas of greater kelp abundance (>25% rock cover). Site DS-11, historically a site with high kelp biomass, had an average *a* of 0.137 m^{-1}. In 2002, *a* values were lower and ranged between $0.076 - 0.138$ m^{-1}. The highest values occurred along the coastline between SDI and Pt. Brower, 0.129 m^{-1} and 0.136 m^{-1}, respectively (Figure 6). However, absorption measurements in the Boulder Patch were noticeably lower in 2002. The largest value was 0.125 m^{-1} near E-3, and DS-11 had an average value of 0.092 m^{-1}, one of the lowest in the entire Boulder Patch.

Trends in scattering (*b*) coefficients were more consistent between years. Higher *b* measurements were always seen in coastal zones near Endicott Island, SDI, and Pt. Brower and gradually decreased with distance from the shoreline (Figures 7 and 8). In 2001, *b* values varied between $1.1 - 13.7$ m^{-1} throughout Stefansson Sound. High coastal values ranged from 13.7 m^{-1} off Endicott Island to 6.6 m^{-1} off Pt. Brower. Scattering values in 2002 decreased, ranging between $0.1 - 7.0$ m^{-1}. Coastal values varied between 7.0 m^{-1} near Endicott Island and 5.1

m^{-1} off Pt. Brower. Lowest b values in both 2001 (1.1 m^{-1}) and 2002 (0.1 m^{-1}) were found offshore near Narwhal Island.

Although water transparency varied between the two sampling periods, greater light attenuation (k) consistently occurred in coastal zones near Endicott Island, SDI, and Pt. Brower, while lower k values were recorded offshore along the eastern and northeastern sides of Stefansson Sound (Figures 9 and 10). In 2001, attenuation ranged from 1.0 - 13.8 m^{-1} throughout Stefansson Sound (Figure 9). Measurements were significantly lower in waters overlying the Boulder Patch ($p = 0.002$) than k values from nearshore waters south of the Boulder Patch. Values were lowest in offshore waters (1.0 – 2.7 m^{-1}) and increased with proximity to the coastline, indicating more turbid water closer to shore. The majority of Boulder Patch, including areas with dense kelp populations (> 25% rock cover), is found predominantly in offshore waters where attenuation measurements were consistently less than 3.6 m^{-1}.

Much lower attenuation coefficients were recorded in summer 2002 than in summer 2001 (Figure 10). The highest values (7.1 – 8.3 m^{-1}) were again recorded near Endicott Island, SDI, and Pt. Brower, but most of Stefansson Sound had measured attenuations less than 6.0 m^{-1}. Similar to 2001, the Boulder Patch was generally characterized by low attenuation measurements (< 2.0 m^{-1}) and had significantly lower k values ($p < 0.001$) than nearshore waters.

PAR measurements collected during summer 2002 followed a typical cyclical pattern with terrestrial surface irradiances peaking between 1200 – 1400 μmoles photons m^{-2} s^{-1} (Figure 11). Surface irradiance maximums were always around 14:00 hr. Starting 5 August, surface irradiance dropped dramatically in conjunction with a series of overcast days. Maximum PAR reached only about 600 μmoles photons m^{-2} s^{-1} during this period. Decreased PAR concentrations continued through 8 August when dataloggers were removed. Underwater sensors also recorded a strong cyclical pattern (Figure 12). The highest PAR values measured by the spherical quantum sensors normally occurred around 14:00 h. and ranged from $100 - 140$ μmoles photons $m^{-2} s^{-1}$. Corresponding to the sudden change in surface irradiance, a large decrease in underwater PAR occurred starting 5 August. Underwater cosine sensors routinely measured downward irradiance between $60 - 80$ μmoles photons $m^{-2} s^{-1}$ until 5 August when downward irradiance declined to levels of $20 - 30$ μmoles photons $m^{-2} s^{-1}$. Apparent increased measurements in underwater PAR levels occurred on all sensors 8 August because dataloggers were removed. Values recorded from both surface and underwater PAR sensors are similar to irradiance measurements made in Stefansson Sound during previous studies (Dunton, 1990).

Total Suspended Solids

Total suspended solids varied greatly throughout Stefansson Sound during summer 2001 ($2.6 - 24.2$ mg L^{-1}). Lower TSS values ($2.6 - 2.8$ mg L^{-1}) were consistently measured in the northeastern sections offshore, near Narwhal Island. Higher values ($23.0 - 24.2$ mg L^{-1}) were located nearshore, adjacent to Endicott Island and SDI, respectively. TSS measurements were significantly lower throughout the Boulder Patch than nearshore waters ($p < 0.001$). We observed a gradual reduction in TSS seaward of the coast toward the northern reaches of Stefansson Sound (Figure 13). Within the Boulder Patch, TSS ranged from 4.2 - 14.3 mg L^{-1}, with a mean of 6.8 mg L^{-1}.

Although TSS concentrations were dramatically lower in summer 2002, the same trends were observed (Figure 14). Highest concentrations ($17.5 - 18.5$ mg L^{-1}) were found near Endicott Island, SDI, and Pt. Brower while lower concentrations (< 1.0 mg L^{-1}) were found offshore near Narwhal Island. Most of the Boulder Patch was located in low turbidity water (i.e., TSS < 4.0 mg L^{-1}), which was significantly lower than coastal waters south of the Boulder Patch (p = 0.001). In both 2001 and 2002, TSS concentrations were significantly correlated with attenuation at 676 nm ($R^2 \approx 0.90$, $p < 0.005$; Figure 15). An analysis of covariance revealed a significant difference between the two years' slopes ($p < 0.05$) indicating different relationships between TSS concentrations and k values measured in Stefansson Sound between years.

Chlorophyll Concentrations

Chlorophyll *a* concentrations ranged from 9.0 to 26.4 μg L^{-1} in summer 2001. The highest concentrations were measured near SDI (24.0 – 26.4 μg L^{-1}). Interpolated chlorophyll data revealed higher concentrations in nearshore areas between Endicott Island and Pt. Brower (Figure 16). Similar chl *a* concentrations were measured in the Boulder Patch at site DS-11 and the surrounding area (19.5 - 20.8 μg L^{-1}). Other sites in Stefansson Sound exhibited relatively lower concentrations (13.0 – 15.0 μg L^{-1}). During summer 2001 there was no significant difference between chlorophyll concentrations taken in nearshore areas versus the Boulder Patch offshore ($p > 0.05$). However, a comparison between chlorophyll *a* concentrations and light attenuation in summer 2001 revealed a significant relationship ($p < .01$).

Chlorophyll *a* concentrations measured in summer 2002 were considerably lower than those measured in 2001. Concentrations ranged from 0.80 – 7.11 μg L^{-1} with the highest concentration occurring near SDI (Figure 17). An interpolation of chlorophyll data revealed that all other sites within Stefansson Sound, including nearshore sampling close to SDI and Endicott Island, exhibited chlorophyll *a* concentrations less than 5.0 μg L^{-1}. Chlorophyll *a* concentrations over the Boulder Patch varied between 2.0 – 4.0 μg L^{-1}. Although Stefansson Sound exhibited lower concentrations in summer 2002, a significant difference (p

< 0.01) was discovered between chlorophyll measurements in the Boulder Patch and those taken in nearshore waters. In summer 2002, there was no significant (p > .05) relationship between chlorophyll a concentrations and light attenuation measured in Stefansson Sound.

Radiative Transfer Equation (RTE) and Productivity Model

IOP data from summers 2001 and 2002 were entered into the RTE to calculate a TSS concentration specific attenuation coefficient [$K^*_d(\lambda,H)$]. Using the $K^*_d(\lambda,H)$, reasonable irradiance estimates for varying TSS concentrations were determined. Once incorporated into the productivity model, kelp production was estimated at fixed TSS concentrations (1, 10, and 20 mg L^{-1}) for the 11 sampling sites over the 60-d open-water period (Table 2). At all sites, greater estimated productivity occurred at lower suspended sediment concentrations (1.0 mg L^{-1}). The lowest estimated productivities at common TSS concentrations occurred at the deepest sites, W-3, W-2, and L-2 (Narwhal Island does not have kelp but was included in Table 2 for comparison), while the largest estimated production occurred at shallower sites, E-1 and E-2. Average estimated production values decreased by an order of magnitude as TSS concentration changed from 1 mg L^{-1} (0.0205 g C gdw^{-1} day^{-1}) to 10 mg L^{-1} (0.0031 g C gdw^{-1} day^{-1}). Assuming a 60-d summer season, this would translate into a change in production from 48.3 g C m^{-2} yr^{-1} to 7.3 g C m^{-2} yr^{-1} in an area of the Boulder Patch where substratum is greater than 25% boulder cover and biomass is equal to 39.3 gdw m^{-2} (Dunton et al, 1982). With exception of the two shallowest sites (E-1 and E-2), increasing TSS concentrations to 20 mg L^{-1} throughout the 60-d summer season would result in negative production values as the metabolic costs of respiration exceed photosynthetic production.

Using the data from the interpolated TSS contours for summers 2001 and 2002 (Figures 13 and 14), production values (g C gdw^{-1} yr^{-1}) were calculated across the Boulder Patch using the unique depths, *in situ* TSS concentrations from the 11 fixed sites (Figure 3), and an arbitrary cloud cover factor of 0.15, chosen to match bottom irradiance values measured in 2002. Estimated production values (g C m^{-2} yr^{-1}) were calculated using biomass numbers reported in Dunton *et al.* (1982). Biomass was 39.3 gdw m^{-2} for areas with rock cover greater than 25% and 10.0 gdw m^{-2} for areas with rock cover of 10-25%. Production estimates for these sites were then interpolated across the Boulder Patch for summers 2001 and 2002 (Figures 18 and 19). During 2001, estimated production ranged from 1.2 to 13.9 g C m^{-2} yr^{-1} (sites E-1 and W-3, respectively). Average production throughout the Boulder Patch was 7.2 g C m^{-2} yr^{-1}. Highest production values were usually in areas with a substratum of > 25% boulder cover. Offshore areas tended to have larger productivity estimates despite increased depths. In 2002, average production increased to 19.5 g C m^{-2} yr^{-1}. Throughout the Boulder Patch, estimated production increased and ranged from 2.4 to 33.3 g C m^{-2} yr^{-1} (sites E-1 and W-1, respectively). Again, productivity was always highest where boulder cover exceeded 25%. The higher estimated production values for 2002 are a direct result of the lower TSS concentrations measured during summer 2002.

Estimated daily production over a range of light regimes and TSS concentrations showed that water transparency has a profound effect on kelp productivity (Figure 20). At a TSS concentration of 13 mg L^{-1}, production was 0.0012 g C gdw^{-1} d^{-1} at half the measured irradiance of 1990; it steadily increased nearly six-fold to 0.0070 g C gdw^{-1} d^{-1} at 1.5 times the measured irradiance. In contrast, production only doubled (0.033 to 0.07 g C gdw^{-1} d^{-1}) between the same irradiance extremes at a TSS of 1 mg L^{-1}. Similarly, modeled production was consistently more sensitive to changes in TSS at lower irradiances. For example, small (10%) increases in irradiance resulted in a 25 – 30% rise in production at 13 mg L^{-1} TSS (Figure 21) at one-half measured insolation. However, at normal or above average insolation values, the percent increase in production was only 10 – 12%. These analyses indicate that kelp production is most sensitive to changes in TSS levels, especially during periods of low summer insolation (i.e. high cloud cover).

Nutrient Concentrations

Ammonium concentrations varied slightly throughout Stefansson Sound in summer 2002. The highest concentrations, 0.26 - 0.29 μM, were measured at DS-11 and E-1, respectively (Table 3). Lower NH_4^+ concentrations (≤ 0.10 μM) were found in northern Stefansson Sound.

Nitrite + nitrate ($NO_2^- + NO_3^-$) concentrations were slightly higher than NH_4^+ concentrations, but were all < 1.0 μM (Table 3). There was little variability in $NO_2^- + NO_3^-$ measurements throughout Stefansson Sound, with concentrations ranging from 0.40 μM at Narwhal Island to 0.59 μM at E-1. With exception of E-1, all sites had measured $NO_2^- + NO_3^-$ concentrations between 0.40 – 0.48 μM.

Ortho-phosphate (PO_4^{3-}) displayed the greatest variation of all nutrients. Concentrations ranged from 1.42 – 5.11 μM (Table 3). The lowest concentration (1.42 μM) was measured at Brower-1, closest to shore. The highest concentrations (4.92 and 5.11 μM) were at sites furthest offshore (W-1 and Narwhal Island, respectively).

Physiochemical Parameters

In summer 2001, surface salinity generally varied between 12.0 – 17.0 psu. Although day-to-day variability was sometimes considerable, mean surface salinity was 12.3 psu with highest values (21.0 – 24.0 psu) recorded off Endicott

25

Island on 1 August 2001 and the lowest values (7.0 – 7.2 psu) recorded on 3 August 2001 along the coast between SDI and Pt. Brower. Surface salinity within the Boulder Patch was relatively constant (11.0 – 13.0 psu) in 2001, with the most northern areas having slightly higher salinities (14.0 – 15.0 psu). Salinity was slightly elevated in summer 2002 compared to summer 2001; average surface salinity was 16.7 psu and ranged between 16.0 – 19.1 psu throughout the Boulder Patch. Generally, surface salinity in Stefansson Sound varied between date rather than site. At all sites except Narwhal Island, surface salinity was highest on 2 August 2002 and lowest on 23 July 2002.

In summer 2001, the average bottom salinity was 22.3 psu and ranged between 18.1 – 30.6 psu. Similar readings were taken in summer 2002; average bottom salinity was 23.3 psu and ranged between 16.7 – 30.0 psu. In both years, highest benthic salinities were recorded at offshore sites (Narwhal Island and W-3), which were also the deepest sites (8.2 and 6.6 m, respectively). Lowest average bottom salinities were measured further inshore, near or at sites E-3 and E-2. Daily fluctuations (2 - 3 psu) occurred mainly in nearshore sites, while deeper, offshore sites remained relatively constant over the study's duration. This trend was observed in both summer 2001 and 2002.

Generally, surface water temperature was elevated close to shore and consistently decreased with increasing distance seaward. In both years, temperatures nearshore were highest, approximately 6.9°C in 2001 and 7.2°C in 2002. Water temperatures were lower in northern Stefansson Sound, about 1.2°C, in both 2001 and 2002. Average sea surface temperature increased throughout the Boulder Patch from 4.0°C in 2001 to 4.8°C in 2002. Though spatial trends were seen in both years, daily fluctuations were also observed both summers, as much as 3.0°C throughout the Boulder Patch in 2002. Average sea surface temperature was warmest on 3 August 2002 (average 7.3°C) and coldest on 26 July 2002 (3.0°C).

In 2001, bottom temperatures varied between -0.9 – 2.7°C. The average benthic temperature was 0.8°C. Bottom temperatures were elevated in 2002, ranging between -1.2 – 4.4°C and averaging 1.6°C. In both years, coldest bottom temperatures were always measured at Narwhal Island but otherwise did not show any geographic trends. Daily fluctuations between bottom temperatures were prominent. In direct contrast with 2002 surface temperatures, coldest bottom temperatures were generally measured on 3 August 2002 (0.2°C) and warmest on 26 July 2002 (3.2°C).

Vertical profiles conducted in 2001 and 2002 revealed the dynamic nature of Stefansson Sound. Daily changes in both temperature (°C) and salinity (psu) were evident throughout the water column, both at shallow inshore sites (E-1; Figure 22) and at deeper offshore sites (Narwhal Island; Figure 24). Most vertical profiles showed a water column predominantly stratified into two distinct layers (Figures 22 - 24). Despite these tendencies, atmospheric conditions and water current dramatically affect water column properties in the area. Comparisons between dates with heavy stratification at similar sites revealed daily temperature changes between 0.0 and 5.0°C and salinity changes between 0.0 and 10.0 psu. On other dates (*eg.* 26 July 2002) the water column is mixed with little temperature or salinity variation. Daily variations in water column properties are a likely indication of turbidity change, ultimately affecting daily kelp production values.

Kelp Growth

Annual *Laminaria solidungula* blade elongation displayed large spatial and temporal variability. Kelp collected in 2001 at DS-11 had an annual blade elongation of 23.0 – 37.0 cm, values comparable to previous studies (Dunton, 1990; Martin and Gallaway, 1994). A mean blade elongation of 23.5 cm characterized the most recent period of growth (GWYR 2000; November 2000 to August 2001) at all sites (Figure 25). During GWYR 2000, five of seven sites had an average increase blade length of 20.0 – 26.0 cm. The other two sites, E-2 and DS-11, grew an average of 12.1 and 37.0 cm, respectively. Specimens at DS-11 consistently had the highest annual elongation. An interannual comparison showed that growth was lowest during the 1999-2000 (GWYR 1999) growth year. With exception of DS-11, blade elongation did not exceed 10.0 cm during this year, suggesting very poor water transparency conditions in summer 1999.

Kelp blade length measurements from specimens collected in summer 2002 confirmed observations from summer 2001 (Figure 26). For example, mean blade elongation for GWYR 2000 was 23.8 cm (compared to 23.5 cm in 2001). In addition, average blade elongation ranged from 20.0 to 26.0 cm at four sites in 2001; at sites E-2, L-2, and DS-11, blade growth for GWYR 2000 was 12.4, 27.9, and 34.3 cm, respectively. We again noted low linear growth during the 1999-2000 growth period, with only specimens collected from DS-11 having an average blade elongation greater than 14.0 cm. The mean blade elongation measured at all sites in GWYR 2001 was 33.8 cm. Additionally, average linear growth was greatest at all sites during GWYR 2001 compared to previous years, and ranged from 39.4 cm at Brower-1 to 23.7 cm at L-2.

Summer 2003 specimens exhibited similar trends as those from summers 2001 and 2002. Blade elongation for GWYR 2002 ranged from 20.0 – 35.2 cm and had an average 28.1 cm (Figure 27). Highest annual linear growth occurred at sites DS-11 and E-1 (35.2 and 33.2 cm, respectively). Unlike other years, sites L-1, L-2, and Brower-1 had reduced elongation compared to other sites. Average elongation for GWYR 2002 (28.8 cm.) was second only to GWYR 2001 (38.8

cm.). Only specimens from DS-11 and E-2 had higher average growth rates in GWYR 2002 than GWYR 2001. Once again GWYR 1999 exhibited reduced elongation compared to other years, and only kelp from DS-11 had elongation measurements greater than 14.0 cm. Average elongation for GWYR 2000 was 21.0 cm, compared to 23.8 cm in GWYR 2002 and 2003.

Discussion

Light Measurements

Each inherent optical property measured demonstrated unique trends in Stefansson Sound. Absorption (*a*), typically affiliated with phytoplankton or dissolved organics (Van Duin *et al.*, 2001; Pegau, 2002), was elevated in waters surrounding Endicott Island and the Boulder Patch in 2001 (Figure 5). Relatively uniform chlorophyll concentrations throughout Stefansson Sound suggest that colored dissolved organic matter (CDOM) may serve an important role. Pegau (2002) found that CDOM could increase arctic nearshore water's absorption properties by 30% in the top 10 m. Highest absorptions were located in areas of the Boulder Patch with greater percentages of rock cover. In previous studies, kelp biomass was routinely higher in areas with the most rock cover (Dunton *et al.*, 1982; Busdosh *et al.*, 1985). This may cause higher humic substance concentrations, which are also affiliated with CDOM (Van Duin *et al.*, 2001). In 2002, *a* was highest in nearshore waters between Pt. Brower and SDI (Figure 6). Increased values occurred over the Boulder Patch as well, but predominantly in areas of low rock cover (E-1, E-2, and E-3).

Typically, scattering (*b*) is affiliated with suspended sediments and organic debris (Van Duin *et al.*, 2001). In 2001, *b* was greatest nearshore and gradually decreased with increasing distance from the shoreline (Figure 7). A similar trend was observed in 2002, although values were substantially lower (Figure 8). Increased *b* near the coast probably results from greater TSS concentrations. As seen in Figures 13 and 14, TSS concentrations are typically highest nearshore. Shallow depths, erosion, and terrestrial runoff are probable causes of elevated suspended sediment and higher subsequent *b* values. Scattering values were substantially greater than absorption values throughout Stefansson Sound (*b:a* > 30), indicating that the system is optically dominated by unconsolidated sediments suspended in the water (Kirk, 1981; 1994). Beam attenuation (k) interpolations were similar to those for b (Figures 9 and 10), and are indicative of high $b:a$ ratios.

Total Suspended Solids

TSS interpolations throughout Stefansson Sound may reflect higher water turbidity characteristic of eroding coastlines. TSS levels measured in 2001 (22.0 – 24.2 mg L^{-1}) along SDI and Endicott Island shorelines were often three to four times higher than those at more seaward locations. TSS concentrations were dramatically lower in 2002, but nearshore concentrations were still significantly higher than offshore waters. The Boulder Patch resides predominately in areas offshore with significantly lower suspended sediment concentrations.

Results show a strong relationship between water column TSS and light attenuation at all measured wavelengths. In both years, high attenuation coefficients and consequent low light penetration were found near SDI and Endicott Island. These appear to correlate with elevated TSS concentrations (compare Figures 9, 10, 13, and 14). Low attenuation (< 3.0 m^{-1}), or high light penetration, corresponded directly to low TSS levels in northern and eastern Stefansson Sound. Offshore waters, typically affiliated with lower TSS values, had higher light penetration through the water column.

Although there was a strong correlation between TSS and attenuation in both years (R^2 = 0.89, p < 0.05), an ANCOVA revealed that the two slopes were not statistically similar. This indicates a different, albeit strong, relationship between TSS and the IOPs between summers 2001 and 2002. There are several possible explanations. Suspended solids include both inorganic and organic detritus that contribute mainly to light scattering but have different optical properties. Zimmerman and Maffione (2000) calculated absorption by inorganic particles in coastal zones to be an order of magnitude lower than values reported for organic detritus (Roessler et al., 1989). Any change in the (in)organic composition of suspended material could alter the relationship between IOPs and suspended material. Several studies have demonstrated the impacts of particle characteristics on optical properties (Blom *et al.*, 1994; Best *et al.*, 2001; Van Duin *et al.*, 2001). Particle size and shape affect fall velocity and the subsequent time particles spend attenuating light in the water column. According to Stoke's law, the fall velocity of any sediment particle is proportional to its square diameter and relative density. Absorption and scattering coefficients are also proportional to the square diameter (Van De Hulst, 1981; Kirk, 1983), and relative density is related to the internal ratio of organic to inorganic material, which influences optical properties as well (Zimmerman and Maffione, 2000). Therefore, significant changes to the amounts of various sized particles may alter IOPs and their relationship to TSS concentrations. Van Duin *et al.* (2001) noted that underwater light conditions in shallow water bodies are predominantly controlled by sedimentation and wind driven resuspension, with changes in wind direction and/or speed causing the majority of temporal variability. Considering the varying and abrupt weather patterns in Stefansson Sound, annual change in suspended sediments' optical properties is expected.

Chlorophyll Concentrations

Chlorophyll *a* concentrations changed dramatically between summers 2001 and 2002 even though measurements remained relatively constant throughout the Boulder Patch during their respective years. In 2001, elevated concentrations ($16.0 - 26.4$ μg L^{-1}) typical of summer open water conditions in Stefansson Sound were measured in nearshore waters (Schell *et al.*, 1982). Measurements throughout the Boulder Patch and further offshore were reduced although not significantly ($p > 0.05$) different from chlorophyll concentrations along the coast. Although chlorophyll *a* concentrations never reached spring bloom conditions common in arctic coastal areas (Alexander, 1974), August sampling occurred well after initial ice cover melt in spring and subsequent nutrient depletion by phytoplankton. Phytoplankton populations likely increase rapidly following ice cover melt in late spring to early summer and gradually decrease throughout summer with nutrient depletion (Schell *et al.*, 1982).

In 2002, chlorophyll *a* concentrations were considerably lower than 2001. Values never exceeded 7.2 μg L^{-1}, and most of Stefansson Sound had concentrations between 2.0 – 4.0 μg L^{-1}, which were lower than those previously recorded (Schell *et al.*, 1982). Chlorophyll *a* concentrations within the Boulder Patch and surrounding offshore waters were significantly ($p < 0.01$) less than those nearshore. Low phytoplankton abundance in summer 2002 may be attributed to reduced freshwater surge from the Sagavanirktok River Delta (Figure 1; Trefry, 2003). Annual outflow from the delta could be a primary source of nutrient enrichment to Stefansson Sound, and reduction of outflow may substantially affect spring and summer phytoplankton populations.

Chlorophyll *a* and light attenuation (*k*) were significantly correlated ($p < 0.01$) in summer 2001 but not in summer 2002 ($p > 0.05$). These results suggest that greater phytoplankton biomass throughout Stefansson Sound in summer 2001 had a significant impact on underwater light conditions while lower phytoplankton biomass in summer 2002 had little impact. Although phytoplankton contribute to absorption and scattering (Van Duin *et al.*, 2001), their cumulative effect on light attenuation may vary with biomass and irradiance (*i.e.* higher biomass may have more effect at lower irradiances). Future chlorophyll measurements in conjunction with optical monitoring may be useful in determining relative importance of phytoplankton to underwater light conditions in the Boulder Patch.

Radiative Transfer Equation (RTE) and Productivity Model

A concentration specific attenuation coefficient [$K^*_d(\lambda,H)$] was developed utilizing IOP and TSS data measured *in situ*. The coefficient allowed reliable estimation of benthic irradiance in systems where suspended sediments are the dominant attenuation source (Maffione *et al*., 2003). Once $K^*_d(\lambda,H)$ was incorporated into the productivity model, production was estimated using previously published photosynthesis vs. irradiance curves (Dunton and Jodwalis, 1988) and calculated PAR levels reaching the canopy. To ensure reasonable estimates, production was calculated at 11 sampling sites (Table 2) under matching abiotic conditions throughout Stefansson Sound. Constant TSS concentrations and surface PAR ensured that the only variable affecting light attenuation between sites is depth (i.e. volume of water absorbing photons between the surface and bottom).

The model results showed that shallower sites always had greater daily productivities. Additionally, daily production measurements at all sites decreased as TSS was increased. These results verified model reasonability and indicate the tremendous influence TSS can have on annual kelp production throughout the Boulder Patch. Under similar photic conditions, an increase in TSS from 1.0 mg L^{-1} to 10.0 mg L^{-1} (TSS values within ranges measured during summers 2001 and 2002) decreased estimated daily production an order of magnitude. At deeper sites, an increase in TSS to 20.0 mg L^{-1} resulted in negative daily production estimates as respiration exceeded photosynthetic production.

Our results clearly demonstrate the important roles of TSS and incident solar irradiance in regulating kelp production. Based on hourly PAR data collected in 1990 – 1991 under a range of TSS levels, we found that increases in modeled daily production coincided with increased surface irradiance, but changes were greatest at lower TSS concentrations. Under higher TSS levels, there was little change in actual production even under intense surface light regimes (Figure 20). These results suggest that changes in surface irradiance, will be most important when TSS concentrations are less than 5 mg L^{-1} (Figure 20).

At lower TSS concentrations, the photosynthetic maximum in adult kelp, P_{max} (42 μmols m^{-2} s^{-1}; Dunton and Jodwalis, 1988), can be attained at lower surface irradiance levels. As surface light levels continuously rise, hours of saturating irradiance (H_{sat}) climb steadily as well. Any increase in surface irradiance beyond P_{max} has no added effects on production; the excess photons are unused. Our productivity model does not account for photoinhibition (reduced photosynthetic production at higher PAR levels). According to Dunton and Jodwalis (1988), daily production could be inhibited beyond 80 μmols m^{-2} s^{-1}. Therefore, kelp production at lower TSS values would continually increase, albeit at reduced amounts, under elevating irradiance conditions until there is an eventual production loss from photoinhibition. However, photoinhibition is unlikely to occur very often, since high TSS loads normally prevent light from reaching levels above 80 μmols photons m^{-2} s^{-1} for extended periods. These results suggest that changes in TSS concentrations will significantly affect annual kelp production in the Boulder Patch over a broad range of summer light regimes.

Using a fixed TSS concentration, daily production can vary substantially based on a combination of surface irradiance and site depth. However, interpolations suggest that TSS concentrations are rarely similar between nearshore and offshore locations. Offshore sites, although located at greater depths, routinely had lower suspended sediment concentrations and higher estimated annual productivities. For instance, estimated production for both summer periods was greater at DS-11, 0.19 g C gdw^{-1} (summer 2001) and 0.78 g C gdw^{-1} (summer 2002), than E-2, 0.16 g C gdw^{-1} (summer 2001) and 0.27 gdw^{-1} (summer 2002), despite DS-11's deeper location. Greater water transparencies, as a result of lower TSS concentrations, facilitate higher irradiance to the bottom at DS-11. Site E-2, although shallower, receives less light due to higher TSS concentrations, which results in less production. This indicates the importance of TSS concentrations during the summer open-water period in determining total annual production throughout the Stefansson Sound Boulder Patch.

Interpolations of biomass dependent production (g C m^{-2} yr^{-1}) indicate greater kelp bed production in offshore areas of the Boulder Patch that are characterized by >25% boulder cover. Regions of 10% and 25% benthic rock cover have less solid substratum needed for kelp establishment, which has significant effects on production per unit area. As a result, the interpolated productivity estimates (Figures 18 and 19) were higher in areas of greater boulder cover. This demonstrates the importance of biomass measurements in providing accurate kelp production estimates. Productivity interpolations completed for this study are based on one-time estimates of biomass reported by Dunton *et al.* (1982). Therefore, the accuracy of these production estimates is difficult to assess. Although estimated production values are slightly higher than those measured in previous studies (Dunton and Schell, 1986), the lack of TSS or canopy light measurements for years of measured *in situ* production makes direct comparison impossible.

Nutrient Concentrations

Kelp growth in arctic nearshore environments has been directly linked to seasonal nutrient fluxes (Chapman and Lindley, 1980; Dunton *et al.*, 1982; Dunton and Schell, 1986; Henley and Dunton, 1997). In many arctic kelp beds, including the Boulder Patch, nutrients are readily available in the winter but are low to undetectable in the summer (Dunton *et al.*, 1982; Schell *et al.*, 1982; Dunton and Schell, 1986; Henley and Dunton, 1997). Nutrient concentrations in summer 2002 were very low and agreed with previously published results from Stefansson Sound (Schell *et al.*, 1982; Dunton and Schell, 1986). Schell *et al.* (1982) found that most available form of inorganic nitrogen, $NO_2^- + NO_3^-$, was usually undetectable but was measured as high as 0.50 μM. Inorganic nitrogen concentrations usually begin to rise in early November following the summer open water period (Chapman and Lindley, 1980). Ortho-phosphate concentrations measured in 1980 ranged from undetectable to 0.60 μM (Schell *et al.*, 1982), dramatically lower than ortho-phosphate concentrations measured in summer 2002.

Physiochemical Parameters

Salinity throughout Stefansson Sound was comparable to values previously recorded (Schell *et al.*, 1982). In 1980, surface salinity in the Beaufort Sea ranged between 13.8 – 29.2‰ and averaged 23.3‰. Salinity further inshore and in the Boulder Patch, was less than 20.0‰. Similar measurements were recorded in Stefansson Sound in 1981 (Schell *et al.*, 1982). Surface salinity in 2001, between 11.0 – 15.0 psu, corresponded to previously published measurements (Barnes *et al.*, 1977; Schell *et al.*, 1982; Dunton, 1990). In 2002, surface salinity in the Boulder Patch increased to 16.0 – 19.1 psu. Higher salinities could be attributed to the reduced outflow of the Sagavanirtok River Delta in spring 2002 (Trefry, 2003), less freshwater to dilute surface salt concentrations in Stefansson Sound.

Bottom salinities varied little between 2001 and 2002 and coincided with values recorded in 1980 and 1981 (Schell *et al.*, 1982). In previous years, salinity in Stefansson Sound was consistently measured at a depth of 6.0 m, and all values were between 26.0 – 30.8‰. Although there was a broader range of bottom salinities in 2001 and 2002 (16.7 – 30.6 psu), this difference could be attributed to depth and measurement location. Many sites in 2001 and 2002 were located near the coast (i.e. E-3, E-2, etc.) and did not exceed 6 m in depth. Shallower depths and proximity to shore likely reduced benthic salinities at deeper, offshore sites (DS-11, Narwhal Island).

Both surface and bottom temperatures from 2001 and 2002 coincided with previous studies. During the summer open-water period, temperatures have been reported between 0.0 – 7.0°C on the surface (Dunton, 1984; Dunton, 1985) and -1.0 – 1.5°C on the bottom (Dunton and Jodwalis, 1988; Dunton, 1990).

Vertical profiles results demonstrate the dynamic nature of Stefansson Sound. Relatively shallow waters in Stefansson Sound are heavily influenced by local weather patterns, and several studies have implicated local weather conditions to changes in subsurface conditions (Dunton *et al.*, 1982; Schell *et al.*, 1982; Busdosh *et al.*, 1985; Dunton and Jodwalis, 1988; Dunton, 1990; Martin and Gallaway, 1994). When stratified, the water column in Stefansson Sound appears to form two distinct layers (Figures 22 – 24). Comparison between previous studies' salinity and temperature data at several depths indicates a similar trend (Dunton *et al.*, 1982; Schell *et al.*, 1982). Vertical structure of the water column in Stefansson Sound should be an emphasis of further study. Optical properties of water in the Boulder Patch may change with various density layers. Additionally, reduction of downward irradiance from either reflection or refraction as light passes through two distinct water masses is still unknown.

Kelp Growth

Linear growth data from Boulder Patch kelp beds provide a valuable baseline for monitoring yearly changes in *Laminaria solidungula* productivity. Current growth data are comparable to previous studies (Dunton, 1990; Martin and Gallaway, 1994) and indicate that the Boulder Patch has maintained kelp bed populations since the construction of the Endicott facility in 1985 (Martin and Galloway, 1994). The substantial decrease, at all sites except DS-11 in kelp blade elongation in the 1999 growth year may reflect reduced water transparency during summer 1999, especially near the shoreline. High light attenuation from elevated TSS levels was most likely the result of a series of major storm events that occurred 18 - 24 August 1999 and again on 2 - 6 October 1999 (Weingartner and Okkonen, 2001; www.wunderground.com). Consistently high blade elongation rates recorded in *L. solidungula* plants collected from DS-11 reflect both the offshore location of this site relative to the other sites and its higher percentage of rock cover (Martin and Gallaway, 1994). Greater rock cover minimizes sediment resuspension. Despite apparently poor water transparency conditions in summer 1999, plant growth rebounded to pre-1999 rates in the 2000 growth year.

Blade elongation data from 2000 to 2002 reflect lower TSS levels and higher water transparency at offshore sites. Almost all sites, except L-2, had an increase in annual linear growth during the 2001 GWYR compared to previous years (Figures 26 and 27). Decreased sediment concentrations measured predominantly offshore during summer 2002, which increased productivity estimates for 2002, agreed with annual linear growth measurements taken from offshore sites (DS-11, E-3, and E-2) in 2003. Other sites maintained similar blade elongations in GWYR 2002 and GWYR 2001 except sites L-1 and Brower-1 and may reflect the sites nearshore locations, shallow depths, and reduced boulder cover. Increased blade elongation from GWYR 2002 and 2001 suggest that a

39

combination of high surface irradiance and/or low average TSS concentrations were present during those two summer seasons.

Model Verification Based on Kelp Growth, TSS, and Irradiance Measurements

A large record, encompassing five years (1980 – 1984) and over 800 observations, was used to determine the quadratic relationship between basal blade length and basal blade dry weight (Figure 28). Using this relationship, basal blade lengths from DS-11 for 1990 and 1991 (22.9 and 23.6 cm respectively; Dunton *et al.*, 1992), were converted to dry weights (2.03 and 2.13 g). Assuming 30% of dry weight is carbon (Dunton and Schell, 1986), total carbon produced in summers 1990 and 1991 would be 0.61 and 0.64 g for an averaged sized specimen, respectively. For kelp at DS-11, calculated productivity from the model using hourly surface irradiance measurements from summers 1990/1991 and modeled TSS concentrations from 2001 was 0.0055 and 0.0054 g C gdw^{-1} d^{-1} for 1 g dry weight, respectively. Over the 120-d summer growth season, the model predicts summer production estimates of 0.64 and 0.66 g C, very similar to calculated production based on blade elongation data (Figure 29). Although *in situ* TSS data was not measured in summers 1990 and 1991, the proximity of production estimates, using modeled TSS from 2001, indicates the potential accuracy of the productivity model using *in situ* hourly irradiance values collected within 7 km of the study site (Dunton *et al.*, 1992).

Subsequently, we compared modeled summer production (g C) with blade elongation data for 2001 and 2002 using the same approach. Integrated values of surface insolation during the same summer periods in 1990, 1991, and 2002 (28 July to 8 August) produced daily averages of 28.90, 24.61, and 28.87 mol photons m^{-2} d^{-1} respectively. Based on the excellent agreement between the measured insolation values in 1990 and 2002, we chose to use the 1990 surface insolation values to estimate kelp production in GWYR 2001 and 2002. For GWYR 2001, mean blade elongation at DS-11 was 34.8 cm based on measurements collected in 2002 and 2003. Using the quadratic relationship between frond length and dry weight, along with 30% carbon content of dry weight (Dunton and Schell, 1986) 1.21 g C was produced during GWYR 2001. Using TSS concentrations measured at DS-11 during summer 2001 and hourly surface irradiance measurements from 1990, modeled production was 1.38 g C (Figure 29). Summer 2002 production estimations were not as accurate. Average blade length for DS-11 was 35.2 cm, which equates to 1.24 g C produced over GWYR 2002. However, model estimates of production for GWYR 2002 were 5.18 g C (Figure 29).

The large discrepancy between measured and modeled productivity for GWYR 2002 is likely related to low TSS values that are not representative of the entire summer. TSS concentrations measured during a two-week period in summer 2002 ($\approx$ 3.0 mg L^{-1} average at DS-11) were three times lower than those measured over the same period in summer 2001 ($\approx$ 9.5 mg L^{-1} average at DS-11; Figures 13 and 14). However, average blade lengths at DS-11 for GWYR 2002 (35.2 cm; Figure 27) were nearly the same as blades lengths for GWYR 2001 (34.8 cm; Figure 26 and 27). This implies that overall light conditions at DS-11 between summers 2001 and 2002 were not significantly different. TSS concentrations may have risen dramatically in summer 2002 following the conclusion of sampling in early August. River discharge studies indicate that some rivers in 2002 refroze after initial ice breakup, a rare event. This phenomenon decreased river discharge rates, affecting normal TSS loads, during our sampling regime in summer 2002 (Trefry, 2003). Photoinhibition may have also played a role since resulting bottom irradiance may have been above the photoinhibition point, 80 μmoles photons m^{-2} s^{-1} (Dunton and Jodwalis, 1988), much of the time. Our model does not account for the losses in production due to photoinhibition. Finally, production equivalent to over 5 g C for an average-sized plant would translate into an average basal blade length of over 60 cm (Figure 28). Kelp of such size were not observed at DS-11 in 2003, indicating that average TSS values for summer 2002 were probably underestimated.

In conclusion, TSS can have variable influences on annual productivity in the Stefansson Sound Boulder Patch. Low summer TSS concentrations will usually result in high annual kelp productivity by increasing the number of hours *Laminaria solidungula* can sustain P_{max}. Any increase in TSS will result in decreased production. Under certain conditions, substantial TSS concentrations and/or low surface irradiance may result in negative production rates, where the metabolic costs of respiration exceed photosynthesis. Comparison of model output with *in situ* blade elongation data indicates that the model does provide reasonable estimates of productivity, but is extremely sensitive to accurate measurements of TSS. Although blade elongation data is subject to less discrepancy than model derived production estimates, using a model precludes extra logistical efforts needed for specimen collection (*i.e.* SCUBA needs, trained personnel). Time spent, costs, and effort are likely comparable between the two methods. Resources spent for underwater collection would be replaced by efforts filtering water and adjusting model calculations. Overall, future monitoring should probably incorporate both methods; collecting kelp periodically (every 2-3 years) and using blade elongation data to verify model derived production estimates for previous years' production.

Future monitoring efforts should continue to focus on the critical linkages between light attenuation (based on the IOP's of the water column), continuous surface irradiance, TSS, and site specific kelp biomass and annual growth. Using these measurements, we can provide nearly instantaneous estimates of kelp productivity using the model we have developed. Site specific biomass would contribute to more accurate estimates of kelp production per unit area across Stefansson Sound and allow more precise comparisons of kelp production in response to both natural and anthropogenic events.

Acknowledgements

We thank the MMS Scientific Review Board, whose constructive criticism of earlier drafts of this report has been very helpful. We also express our sincere appreciation to the following BP employees for their logistical support and for maintaining a safe working environment at BP Endicott: Bill Streever, Stan Gates, Troy Weiss, Henry Harrington, Jerry Ferguson, Rocky Jones, Royce O'Brien, and Vince Volpe. We thank Steve Schreiber and Brian Stevens for the continuous use of their water treatment lab and Ted Dunton and John Dunton for their mechanical expertise. We especially appreciate the kindness and hospitality extended to us by the entire Endicott facility of BP Exploration, Alaska. Without the joint financial and logistical support provided by BP and MMS, this study would not have been possible.

Literature Cited

Alexander, V. 1974. Primary productivity regimes of the nearshore Beaufort Sea, with reference to potential roles of ice biota. pgs. 609-635. *In*: J.C. Reed and J.E. Sater (eds.), The Coast of Shelf of the Beaufort Sea. Arctic Inst. N. Am., Arlington, VA.

Alexander, H.D. and K.H. Dunton. 2002. Freshwater inundation effects on emergent vegetation of a hypersaline salt marsh. *Estuaries* 25: 1426-1435.

Barnes, P.W., E. Reimnitz, and D. McDowell. 1977. Current meter and water level observations in Stefansson Sound, Summer, 1976. *In*: Miscellaneous Hydrologic and Geologic Observations on the Beaufort Seas Shelf, Alaska. U.S. Geological Survey open file report 77-477. B1-B7.

Best, E.P.H., C.P. Buzzelli, S.M. Bartell, R.L. Wetzel, W.A. Boyd, R.D. Doyle, and K.R. Campell. 2001. Modeling submersed macrophyte growth in relation to underwater light climate: modeling approaches and application potential. *Hydrobiologia* 444: 43-70.

Blom G., E.H.S. Van Duin, and L. Lijklema. 1994. Sediment resuspension and light conditions in some shallow Dutch lakes. *Water Science and Technology* 30: 243-252.

Burd, A.B. 2003. Boulder Patch kelp model: draft report. Technical report, Department of Marine Sciences, University of Georgia.

Busdosh, M., C.L. Beehler, G.A. Robilliard, and K.R. Tarbox. 1985. Distribution and abundance of kelp in the Alaskan Beaufort Sea near Prudhoe Bay. *Arctic* 38(1): 18-22.

Butler, B. 1998. "Precipitable water at kp – 1993-1998". MMA Memo No. 238, 1998.

Chapman, A.R. and J.E. Lindley. 1980. Seasonal growth of *Laminaria solidungula* in the Canadian High Arctic in relation to irradiance and dissolved nutrient concentrations. *Marine Biology*. 57: 1-5.

Di Toro, D.M. 1978. Optics of turbid estuarine waters: approximations and applications. *Water Research* 12: 1059-1068.

Dunton, K.H., E. Reimnitz, and S. Schonberg. 1982. An arctic kelp community in the Alaskan Beaufort Sea. *Arctic* 35(4): 465-484.

Dunton, K.H. 1984. An annual carbon budget for an arctic kelp community. *In*: P. Barnes, D. Schell, and E. Reimnitz (eds.). The Alaskan Beaufort Sea – Ecosystems and Environment. Orlando: Academic Press. 311-326.

Dunton, K.H. 1985. Growth of dark-exposed *Laminaria saccharina* (L.) Lamour and *Laminaria solidungula* (J.) Ag. (Laminariales, Phaeophyta) in the Alaskan Beaufort Sea. *Journal of Experimental Marine Biology and Ecology* 94: 181-189.

Dunton, K.H. 1990. Growth and production in *Laminaria solidungula*: relation to continuous underwater light levels in the Alaskan High Arctic. *Marine Biology* 106: 297-304.

Dunton, K.H. and D.M. Schell. 1986. A seasonal carbon budget for the kelp *Laminaria solidungula. Limnology and Oceanography* 42(2): 209-216.

Dunton, K.H. and C.M. Jodwalis. 1988. Photosynthetic performance of *Laminaria solidungula* measured *in situ* in the Alaskan High Arctic. *Marine Biology* 98:277-285.

Dunton, K.H., S.V. Schonberg, and L.R. Martin. 1992. Linear growth, tissue density, and carbon content in *Laminaria solidungula. In*: Endicott Beaufort Sea Boulder Patch Monitoring Program (1984 – 1991). Final Report: LGL Ecological Research Associates, Inc. 3-1.

ESRI, Inc. 1999. ArcView 3.2. Redlands, California.

Gregg W.W. and K.L. Carder. 1990. A simple spectral solar irradiance model for cloudless marine atmospheres. *Limnology and Oceanography* 35: 1657-1675.

Henley, W.J. and K.H. Dunton. 1995. A seasonal comparison of carbon, nitrogen, and pigment content in *Laminaria solidungula* and *L. saccharina* (Laminariales, Phaeophyta) in the Alaskan Arctic. *Journal of Phycology* 31: 325-331.

Henley, W.J. and K.H. Dunton. 1997. Effects of nitrogen supply and seven months of continuous darkness on growth and photosynthesis of the arctic kelp, *Laminaria solidungula*. *Limnology and Oceanography* 42(2): 209-216.

Hooper, R.G. 1984. Functional adaptations to the polar environment by the arctic kelp, *Laminaria solidungula*. *British Phycological Journal* 19: 194.

Hopkins, D.M. 1979. The Flaxman formation on northern Alaska: record of early Wisconsinan shelf glaciation in the High Arctic? "XIVth Pacific Science Congress, Khabarovsk". Abstracts volume: 15-16.

Jassby, A. and T. Platt. 1976. Mathematical formulation of the relationship between photosynthesis and light for phytoplankton. *Limnology and Oceanography* 21: 540-547.

Kirk, J.T.O. 1981. Monte Carlo study of the nature of the underwater light field in, and the relationships between optical properties of, turbid yellow waters. *Australian Journal of Marine Freshwater Research* 32(4): 517-532.

Kirk, J.T.O. 1983. Light and Photosynthesis in Aquatic Ecosystems. Cambridge University Press, Cambridge. 12-13.

Kirk, J.T.O. 1984a. Dependence of relationship between inherent and apparent optical properties of water on solar altitude. *Limnology and Oceanography* 29(2): 350-356.

Kirk, J.T.O. 1984b. Attenuation of solar radiation in scattering-absorbing waters: a simplified procedure for its calculation. *Applied Optics* 23(21): 3737-3739.

Kirk, J.T.O. 1994. Characteristics of the light field in highly turbid waters; A Monte Carlo study. *Limnology and Oceanography* 39(3): 702-706.

47

Kirst, G.O. and C. Wiencke. 1995. Ecophysiology of polar algae. *Journal of Phycology* 31: 181-199.

Kondratyev, K.Y. 1954. Radiant solar energy [In Russ.]. Leningrad. [cited after Kirk (1983)].

Lüning, K. and M.J. Dring. 1979. Continuous underwater light measurement near Helgoland (North Sea) and its significance for characteristic light limits in the sublittoral region. *Helgolander wiss. Meeresunters.* 32: 403-424.

MacCarthy, G.R. 1958. Glacial boulder on the arctic coast of Alaska. *Arctic* 11: 71-86.

Maffione, R.A., 1998. Theoretical developments on the optical properties of highly turbid waters and sea ice. *Limnology and Oceanography* 43: 29-33.

Maffione, R.A. 2003. Boulder Patch Optical Model: Preliminary Model. Technical report, HOBI Laboratories.

Maffione, R.A., J. Kaldy, and L. Cifuentes. 2003. Semi-empirical model of the benthic spectral-downwelling irradiance in high suspended sediment environments. *Estuaries*. in press.

Martin, L.R. and B.J. Gallaway. 1994. The effects of the Endicott Development Project on the Boulder Patch, an arctic kelp community in Stefansson Sound, Alaska. *Arctic* 47(1): 54-64.

The Mathworks, Inc. 2000. Matlab 6.1. Natick, Massachusetts.

Parsons, T.R., Y. Maita, and C.M. Lalli. 1984. *In*: <u>A Manual of Chemical and Biological Methods for Seawater Analysis</u>. Oxford: Pergamon Press. 107-109.

Pegau, W.S. 2002. Inherent optical properties of the central arctic surface waters. *Journal of Geophysical Research* 107(C10): 1995-1999.

Platt, T., C.L. Gallegos, and W.G. Harrison. 1980. Photoinhibition of photosynthesis in natural assemblages of marine phytoplankton. *Journal of Marine Research* 38: 687-701.

Primer-E Ltd. 2001. Primer v5. Plymouth Marine Laboratory, Plymouth, UK.

Roessler, C.S., M.J. Perry, and K.L. Carder. 1989. Modeling *in situ* phytoplankton absorption from total absorption spectra in productive inland marine waters. *Limnology and Oceanography* 34: 1510-1523.

Schell D.M., P.J. Ziemann, D.M. Parrish, K.H. Dunton, and E.J. Brown. 1982. "Foodweb and nutrient dynamics in nearshore Alaska Beaufort Sea waters". Draft final report, Institute of Water Resources, University of Alaska Fairbanks.

SPSS Inc. 2000. SPSS 10.0. Chicago, Illinois.

Trefry, J.H. 2003. "River loading and the bifurcated breakup". ANIMIDA task 5 final report, Minerals Management Service. Anchorage, Ak.

Van Duin, E.H., G. Blom, F.J. Los, R. Maffione, R. Zimmerman, C.F. Cerco, M. Dortch, and E.P Best. 2001. Modeling underwater light climate in relation to sedimentation, resuspension, water quality and autotrophic growth. *Hydrobiologica* 444: 25-42.

Van De Hulst, H.C. 1957. Light Scattering by Small Particles. New York. John Wiley & Sons, Inc. 3-5.

Weingartner, T.J. and S.R. Okkonen. 2001. "Beaufort Sea nearshore under-ice currents: Science, analysis and logistics". OCS Study MMS 2001-068.

Welschmeyer, N.A. 1994. Fluorometric analysis of chlorophyll *a* in the presence of chlorophyll b and pheopigments. *Limnology and Oceanography* 39(8): 1985-1992.

Zimmerman, R.C. and R.A. Maffione. 2000. Radiative transfer and photosynthesis of aquatic vegetation in turbid coastal waters. *Hydrobiologia*: in press.

Table 1. Terminology and Units.

Term	Description	Units
IOPs	Inherent Optical Properties; a term characterizing the absorption, scattering, and attenuation of a particular area	---
PAR	Photosynthetically Active Radiation; total radiation in the 400 to 700 nm wavelength interval	μmols photons m^{-2} s^{-1}
TSS	Total Suspended Solids; measure of the amount of non-dissolved material in water column	$mg\ L^{-1}$
RTE	Radiative Transfer Equation; equation used to determine spectral irradiance at any given depth	---
Absorption (a)	Fraction of radiant energy absorbed from light per unit distance passed through water column	m^{-1}
Scattering (b)	Fraction of radiant energy reflected from light per unit distance passed through the water column	m^{-1}
Light Attenuation (k)	Fraction of radiant energy removed from light per unit distance passed through the water column by either absorption or scattering	m^{-1}
$K_d(\lambda,H)$	Bulk Downwelling Irradiance Attenuation Coefficient; Fraction of irradiance removed per unit distance passed through the water column by depth H	m^{-1}
H_{sat}	Number of hours that *L. solidungula* is exposed to PAR that meets or exceeds the minimum irradiance to produce maximum photosynthetic production	hrs
H	Depth of measurement	m
$E_d(\lambda,0^+)$ or $E_d(\lambda,H)$	Downwelling Spectral Irradiance Incident; Likely amount of spectral irradiance occurring on the water's surface (0^+). An H denotes spectral irradiance reaching depth H	$W\ m^{-2}$
C_{TSS}	Total beam attenuation at a specific TSS	m^{-1}
$K^*_d(\lambda,H)$	Concentration Specific Attenuation Coefficient; Fraction of radiant energy removed per unit distance by depth H (by either absorption or scattering) based on the concentration of suspended solids	m^{-1}
GWYR	Growth Year; Period beginning 15th November one year and ending 15th November the following year	yr

Table 2. Productivity model estimates of daily production at eleven
locations within Stefansson Sound Boulder Patch over a 60-d.
summer period at fixed TSS concentrations of 1, 10, and 20 mg
L^{-1}. Note: negative production denotes respiration costs
exceeding photosynthetic production.

Site	Depth (m)	Production (g C gdw^{-1} day^{-1})			% decrease from 1.0 to 20.0 mg L^{-1}
		1.0 mg L^{-1} of TSS	10.0 mg L^{-1} of TSS	20.0 mg L^{-1} of TSS	
Narwhal Island	8.2	0.0177	0.0005	-0.0005	103
W-3	6.6	0.0196	0.0018	-0.0004	102
W-2	6.2	0.0200	0.0022	-0.0003	102
L-2	6.2	0.0200	0.0022	-0.0003	102
DS-11	6.1	0.0202	0.0023	-0.0003	101
W-1	6.0	0.0203	0.0025	-0.0003	101
L-1	5.5	0.0210	0.0033	-0.0001	100
E-3	5.5	0.0210	0.0033	-0.0001	100
Brower-1	5.4	0.0211	0.0035	-0.0001	100
E-1	4.4	0.0222	0.0061	0.0006	97
E-2	4.3	0.0223	0.0064	0.0006	97

Table 3: Average NH_4^+, $NO_2^- + NO_3^-$, and PO_4^{3-} concentrations (μM) measured at six sites within Stefansson Sound during summer 2002.

Sites	NH_4^+ (μM)	$NO_2^- + NO_3^-$ (μM)	PO_4^{3-} (μM)
W-1	0.05 ± 0.01	0.44 ± 0.04	4.92 ± 0.54
W-3	0.10 ± 0.01	0.45 ± 0.01	2.40 ± 1.07
Narwhal (2 meters)	0.11 ± 0.01	0.42 ± 0.01	3.99 ± 2.25
Narwhal (8 meters)	0.12 ± 0.11	0.40 ± 0.04	5.11 ± 1.31
DS-11	0.26 ± 0.24	0.48 ± 0.12	3.03 ± 2.01
E-1	0.29 ± 0.04	0.59 ± 0.11	3.11 ± 0.18
Brower-1	0.18 ± 0.18	0.44 ± 0.11	1.42 ± 0.89

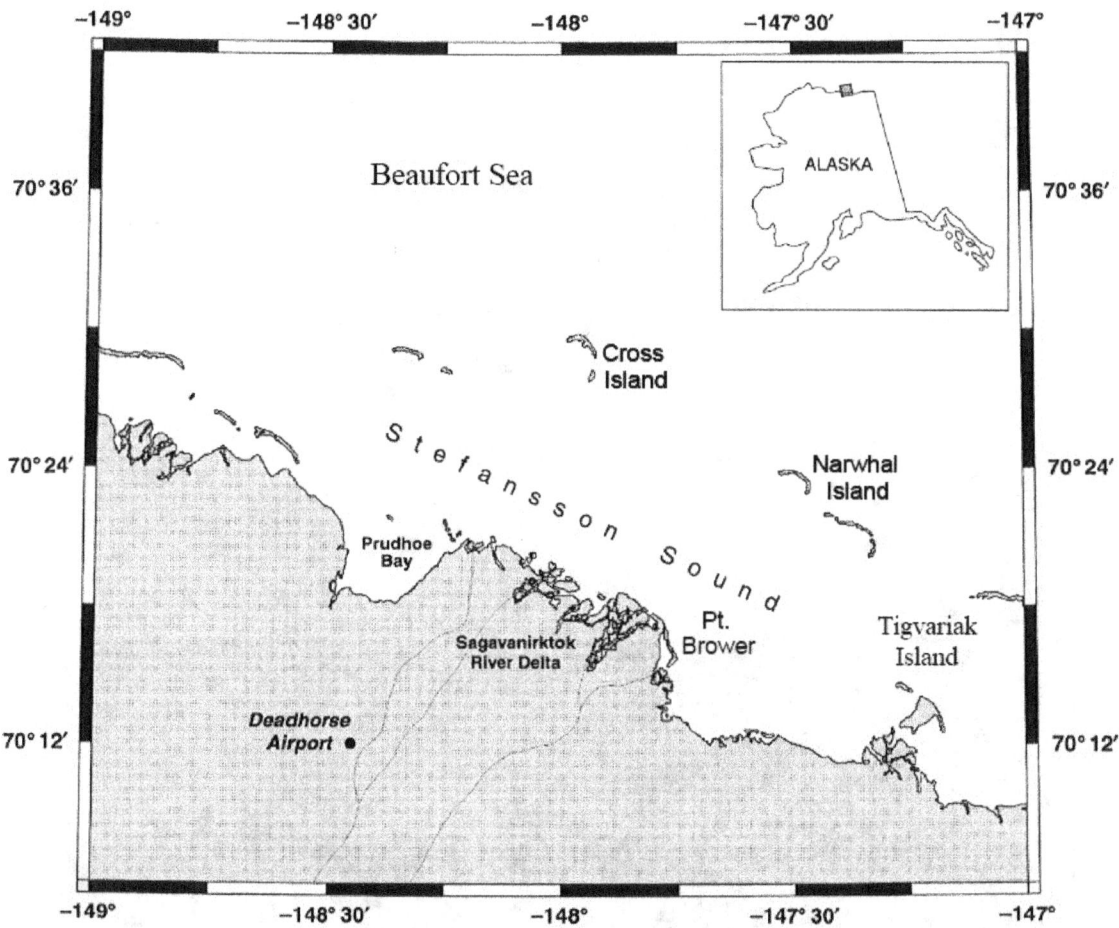

Figure 1. Location of Stefansson Sound, Alaska (adapted from
Weingartner and Okkonen, 2001).

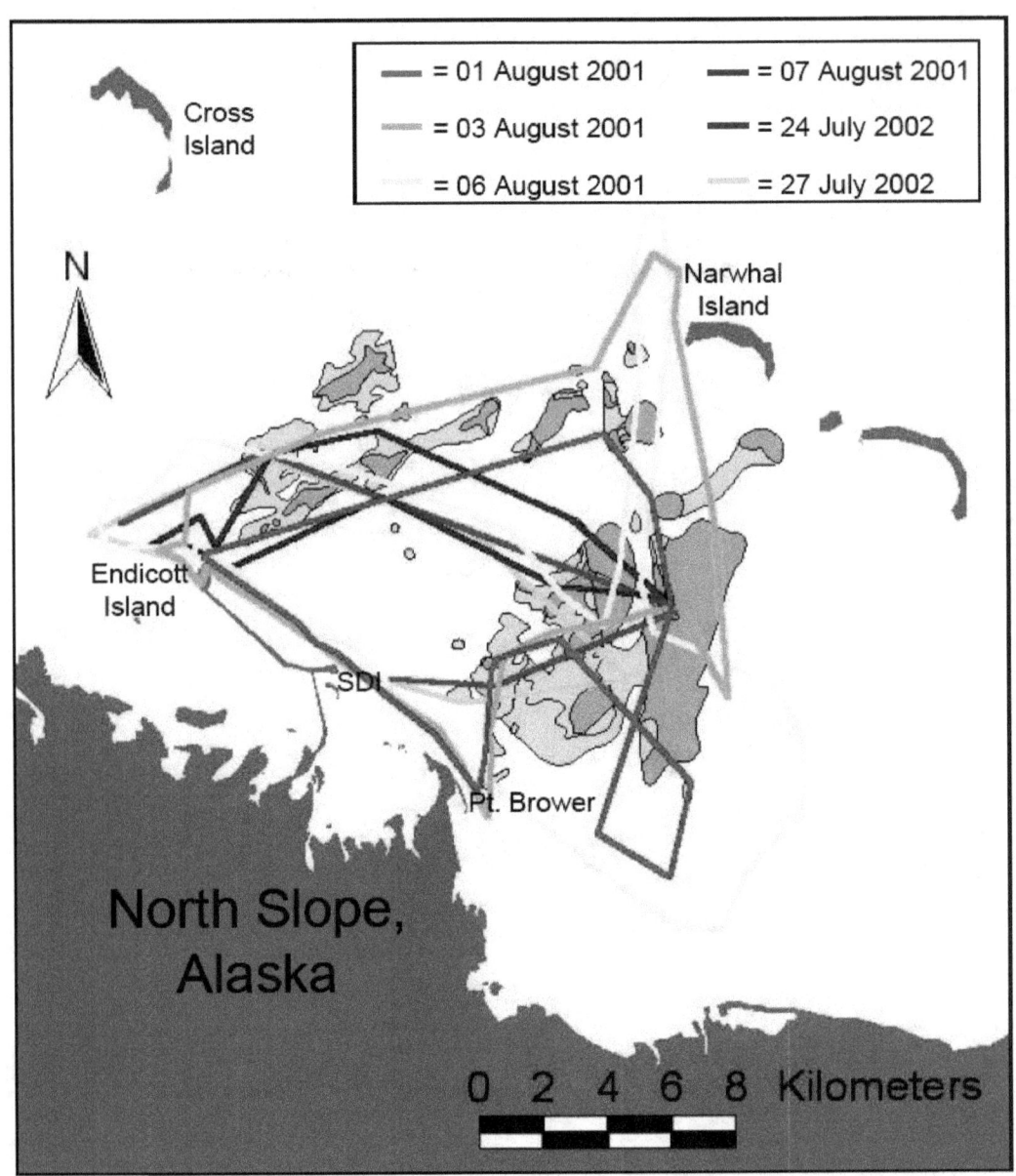

Figure 2. Tracklines for ac-9 and CTD tows conducted during August 2001 and July 2002. Grey shaded areas represent seabed boulder and cobble distribution based on geologic surveys conducted in 1980 and 1999 (Hopkins, 1979; Dunton *et al.*, 1982). Dark grey represents areas of boulder cover > 25%. Light grey represents areas of boulder cover between 10% - 25%.

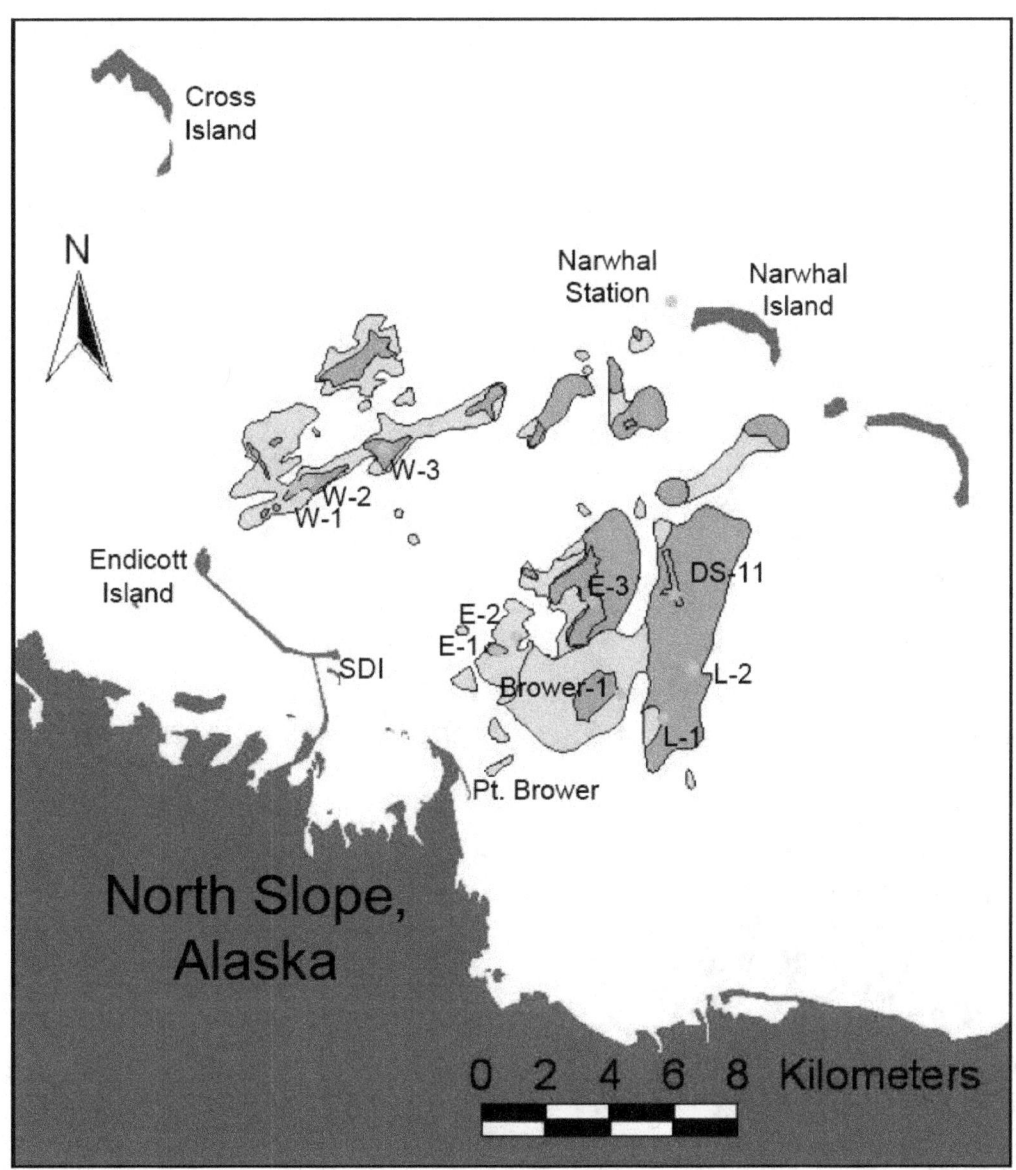

Figure 3. Sites where vertical profiles were measured in summer 2001 and 2002.
Grey shaded areas represent Boulder Patch extent based on geologic
surveys conducted in 1980 and 1999 (Hopkins, 1979; Dunton *et al.*,
1982). Dark grey represents areas of boulder cover > 25%. Light grey
represents areas of boulder cover between 10% - 25%.

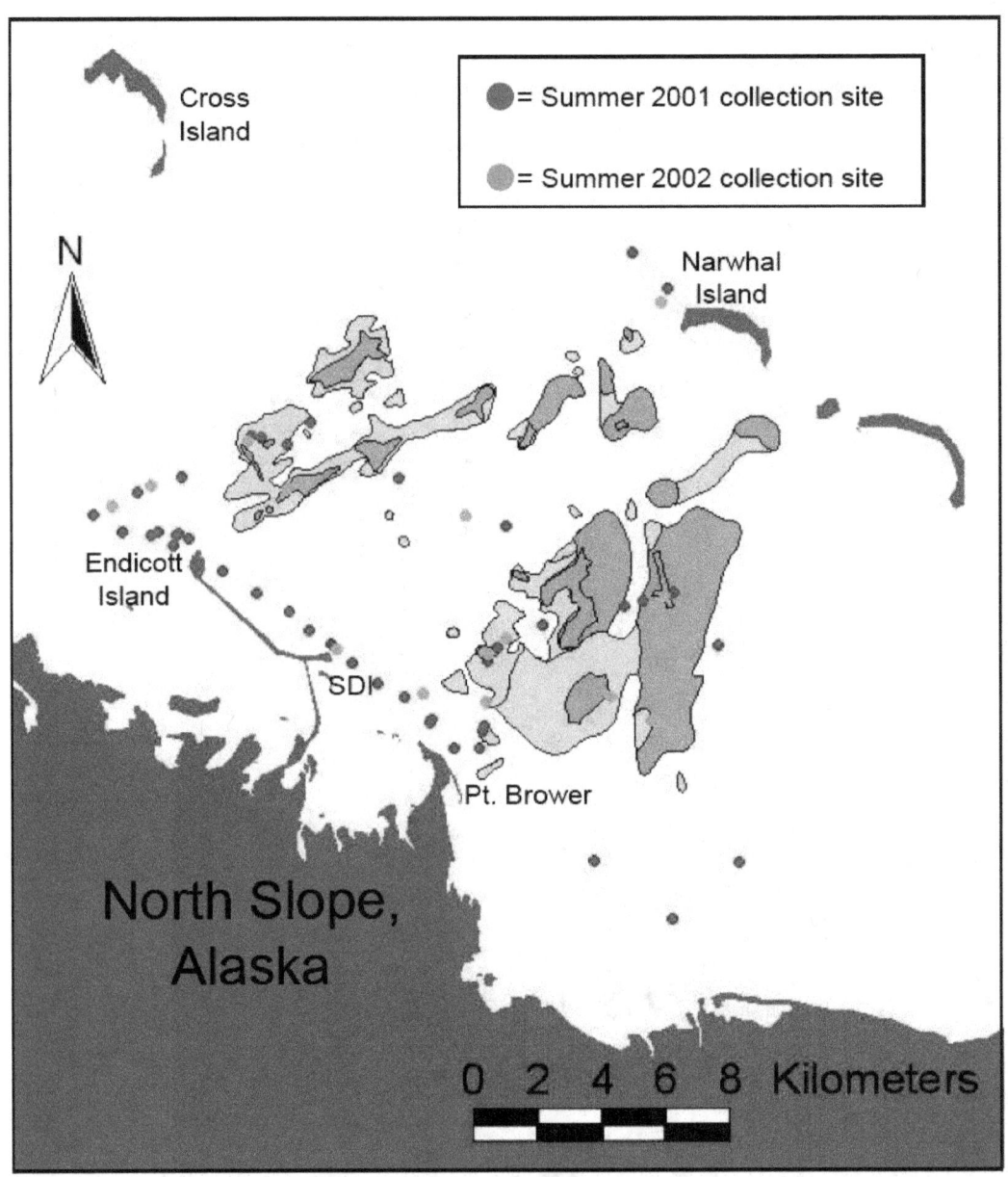

Figure 4. Locations of Summer 2001 and 2002 water collection sites for TSS
          and chlorophyll *a* measurement. Grey shaded areas represent extent of
          Boulder Patch based on geologic surveys conducted in 1980 and 1999.
          Dark grey represents areas of boulder cover > 25%. Light grey
          represents areas of boulder cover between 10% - 25%.

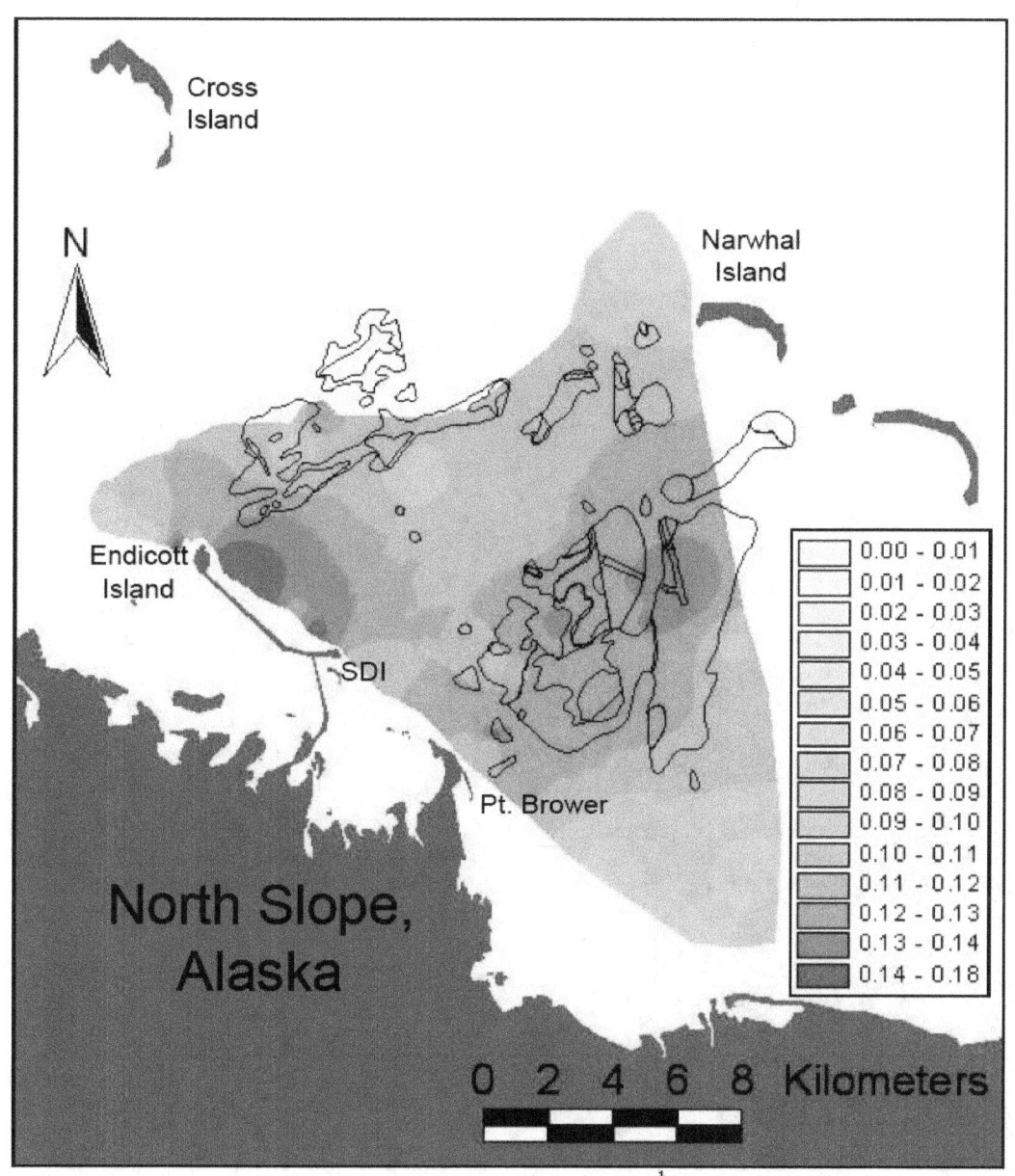

Figure 5. Interpolated absorption coefficients (m^{-1}) at 676 nm for summer 2001.
Areas of > 10% boulder cover are outlined in black.

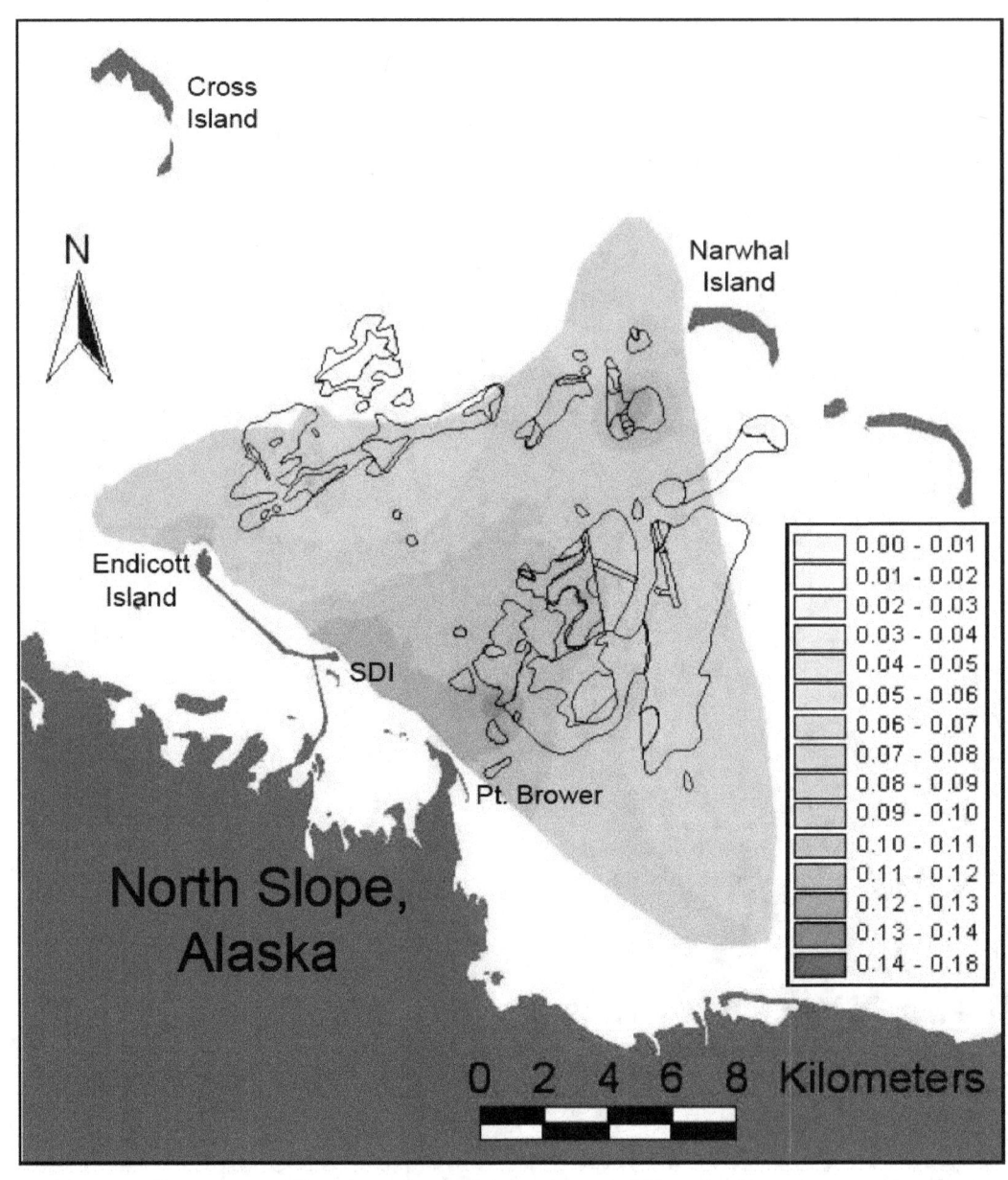

Figure 6. Interpolated absorption coefficients (m^{-1}) at 676 nm for summer 2002. Areas of > 10% boulder cover are outlined in black.

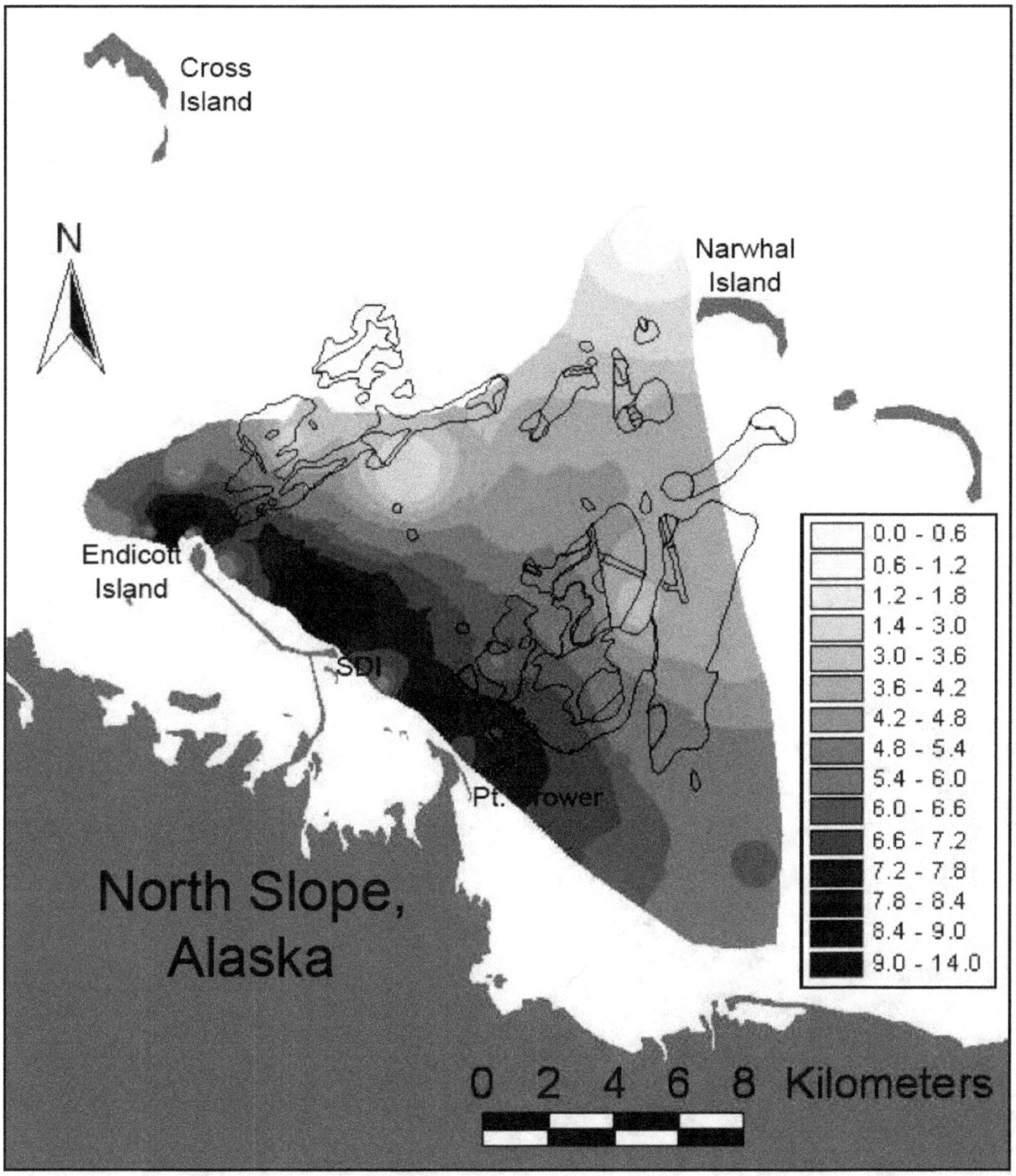
Cross
Island
N
Narwhal
Island
Endicott
Island
SDI
Pt. Brower
North Slope,
Alaska
0.0 - 0.6
0.6 - 1.2
1.2 - 1.8
1.4 - 3.0
3.0 - 3.6
3.6 - 4.2
4.2 - 4.8
4.8 - 5.4
5.4 - 6.0
6.0 - 6.6
6.6 - 7.2
7.2 - 7.8
7.8 - 8.4
8.4 - 9.0
9.0 - 14.0
0 2 4 6 8 Kilometers

Figure 7. Interpolated scattering coefficients (m^{-1}) at 676 nm for summer 2001. Areas of > 10% boulder cover are outlined in black.

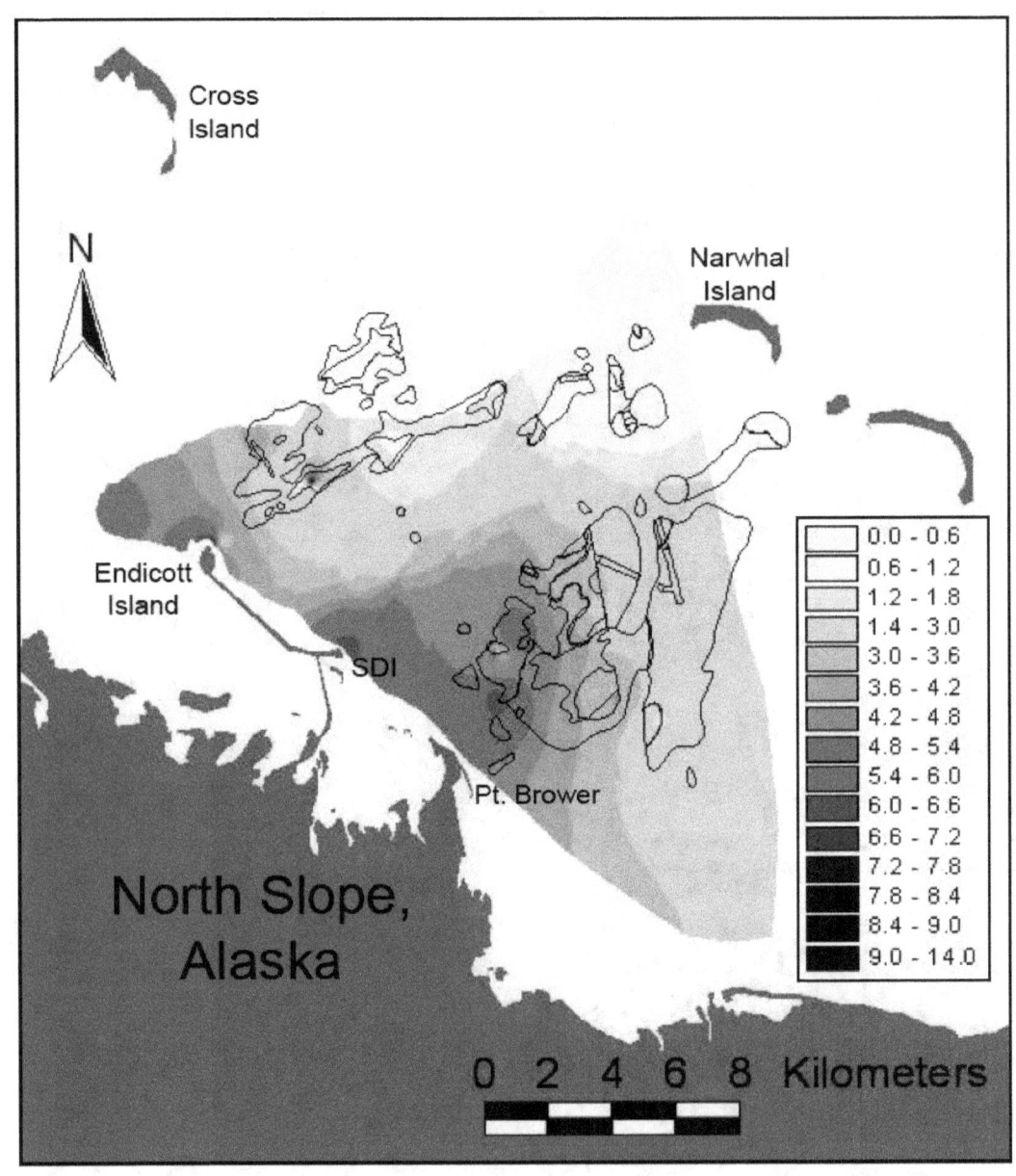

Figure 8. Interpolated scattering coefficients (m^{-1}) at 676 nm for summer 2002. Areas of > 10% boulder cover are outlined in black.

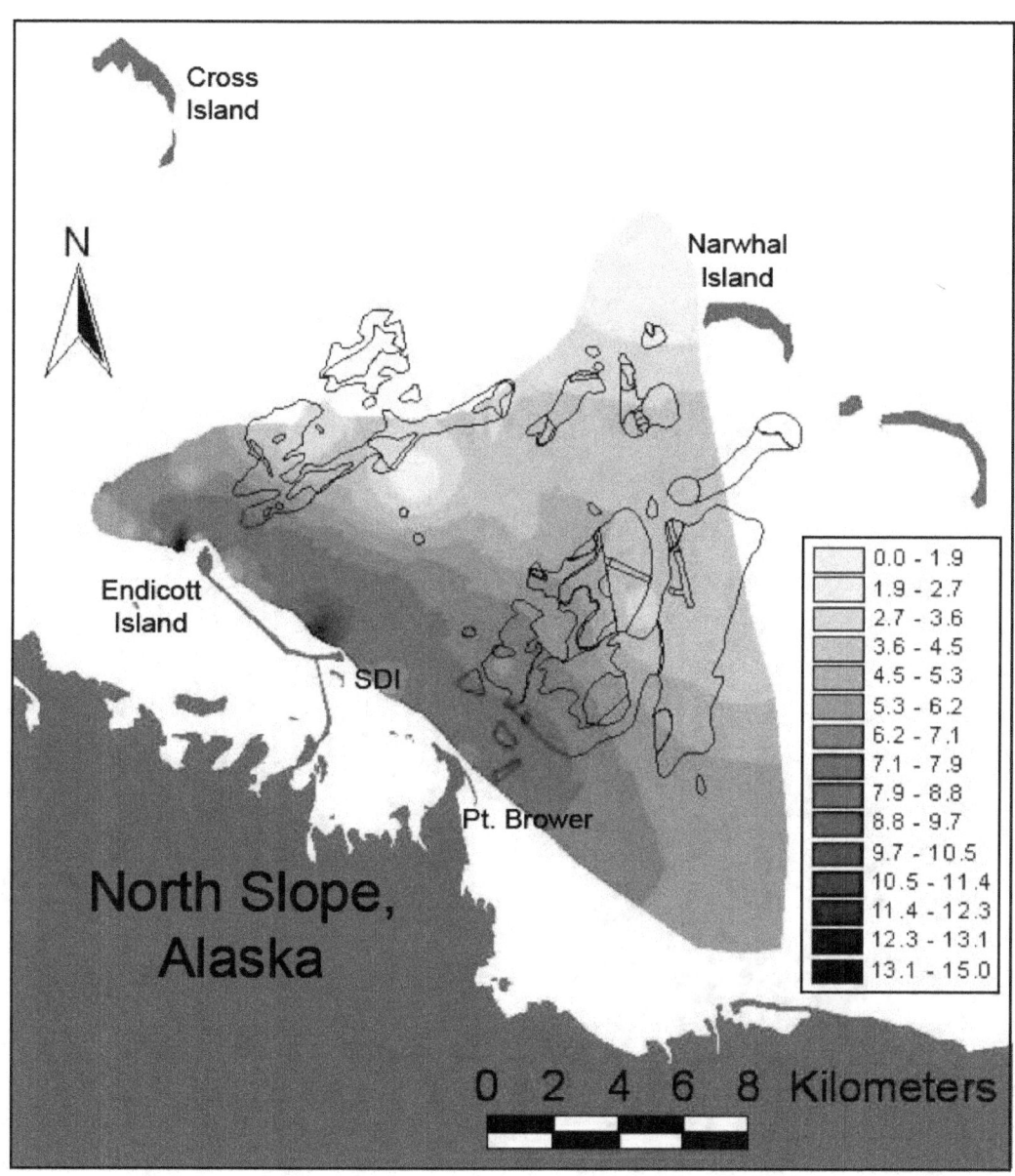

Figure 9. Interpolated beam attenuations (m^{-1}) at 676 nm for summer 2001.
Areas of > 10% boulder cover are outlined in black.

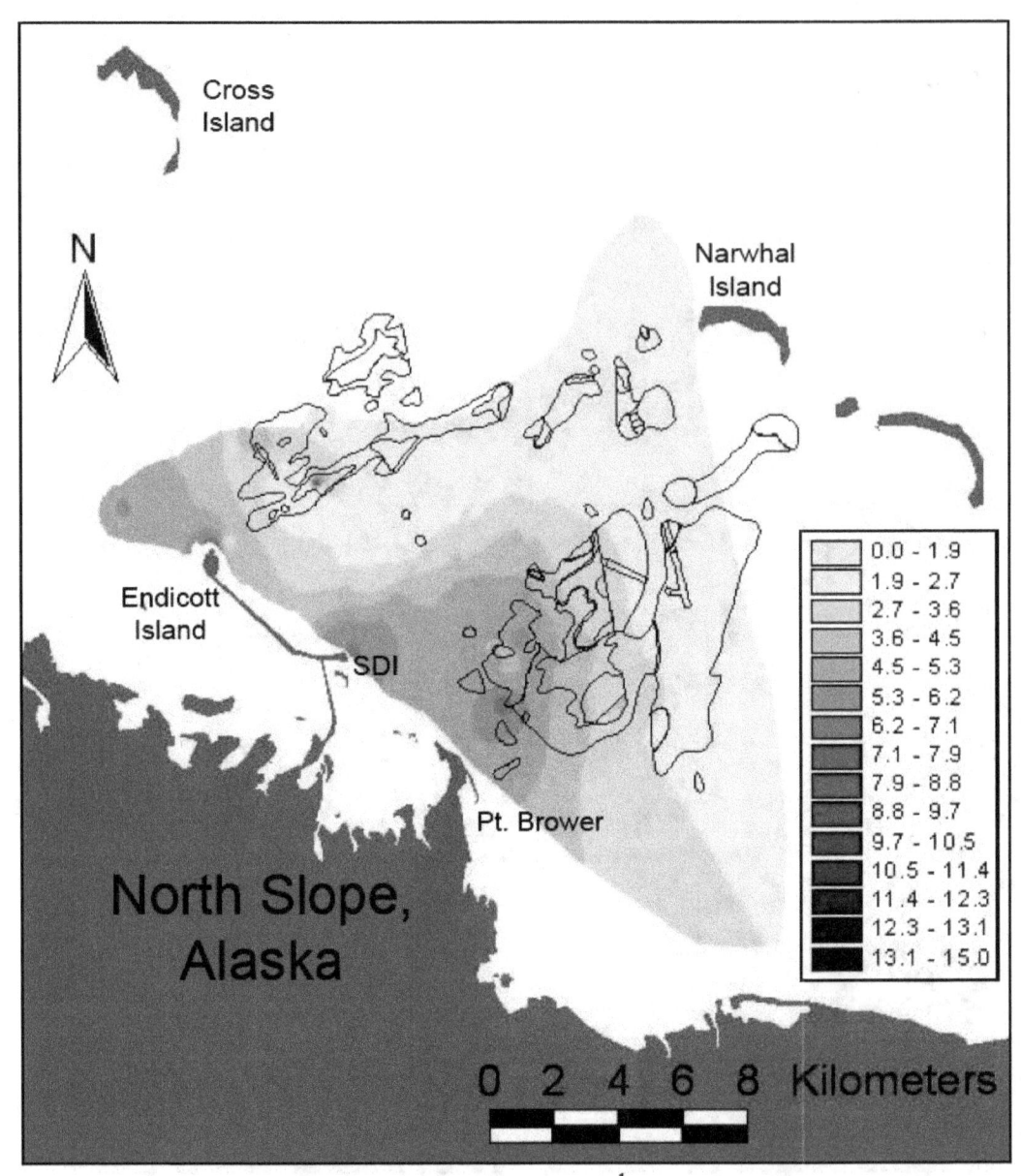

Figure 10. Interpolated beam attenuations (m^{-1}) at 676 nm for summer 2002.
Areas of > 10% boulder cover are outlined in black

63

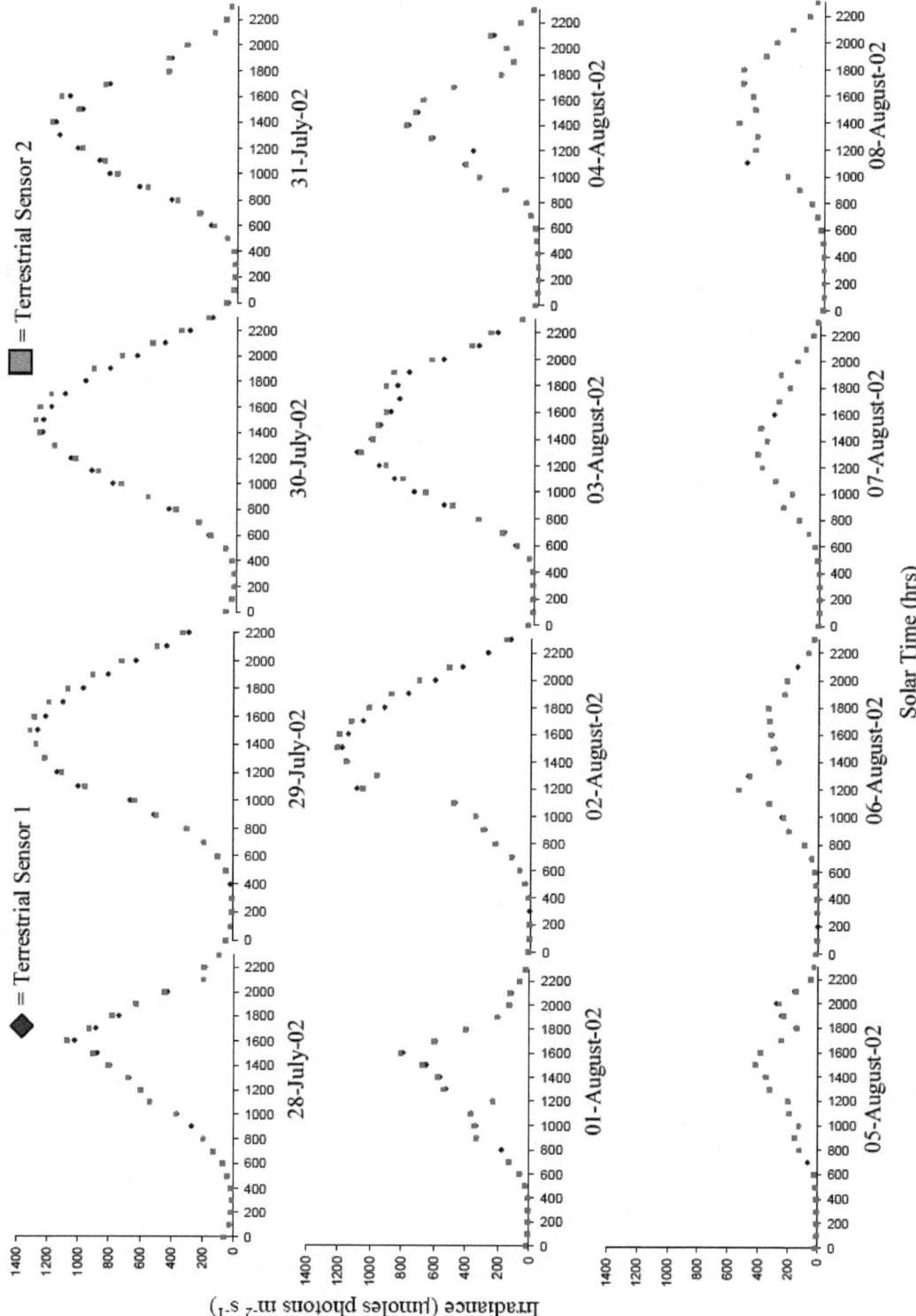

Figure 11. Daily surface irradiance measurements from 28 July to 8 August 2002.

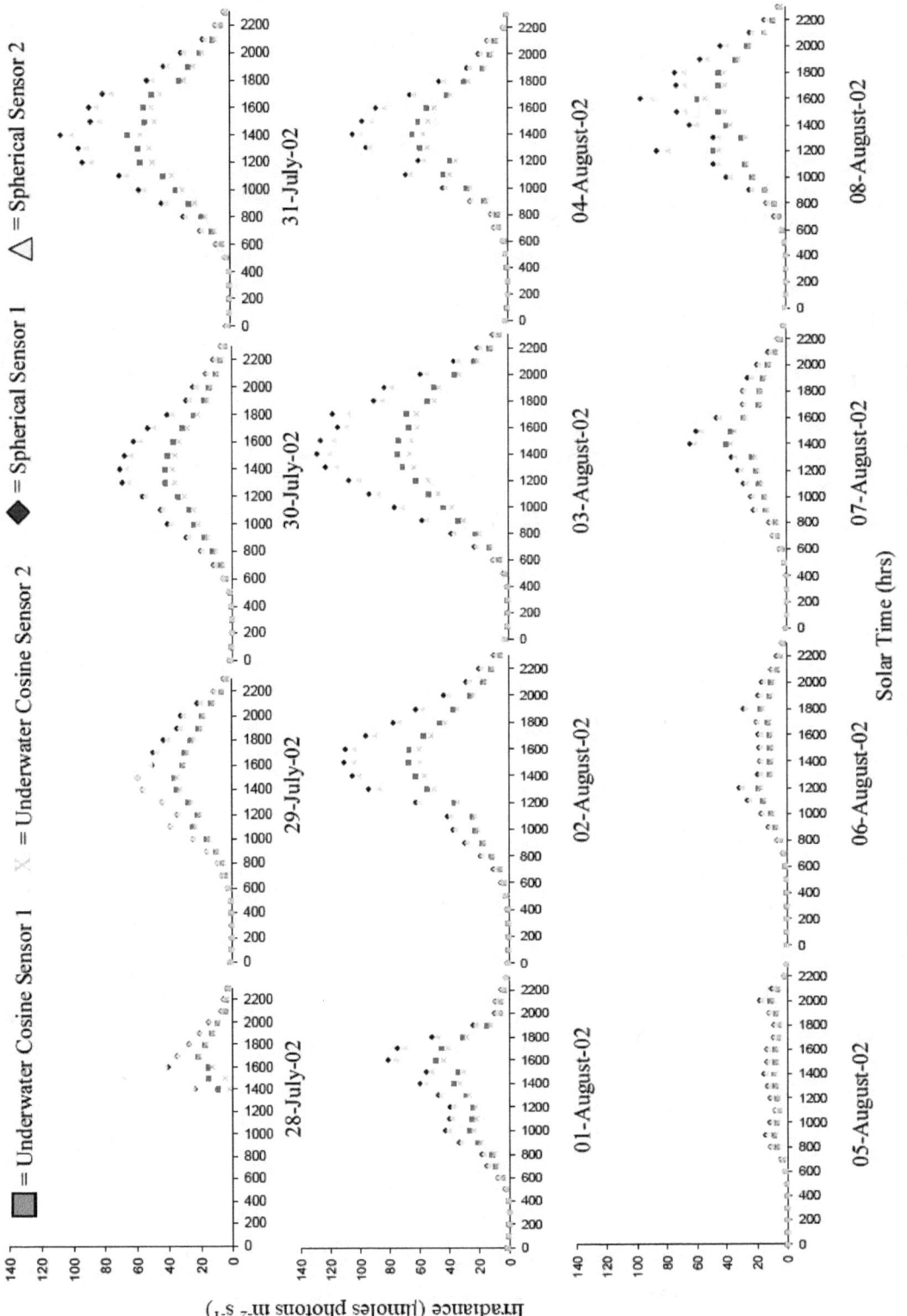

Figure 12. Daily underwater irradiance measurements from 28 July to 8 August 2002.

64

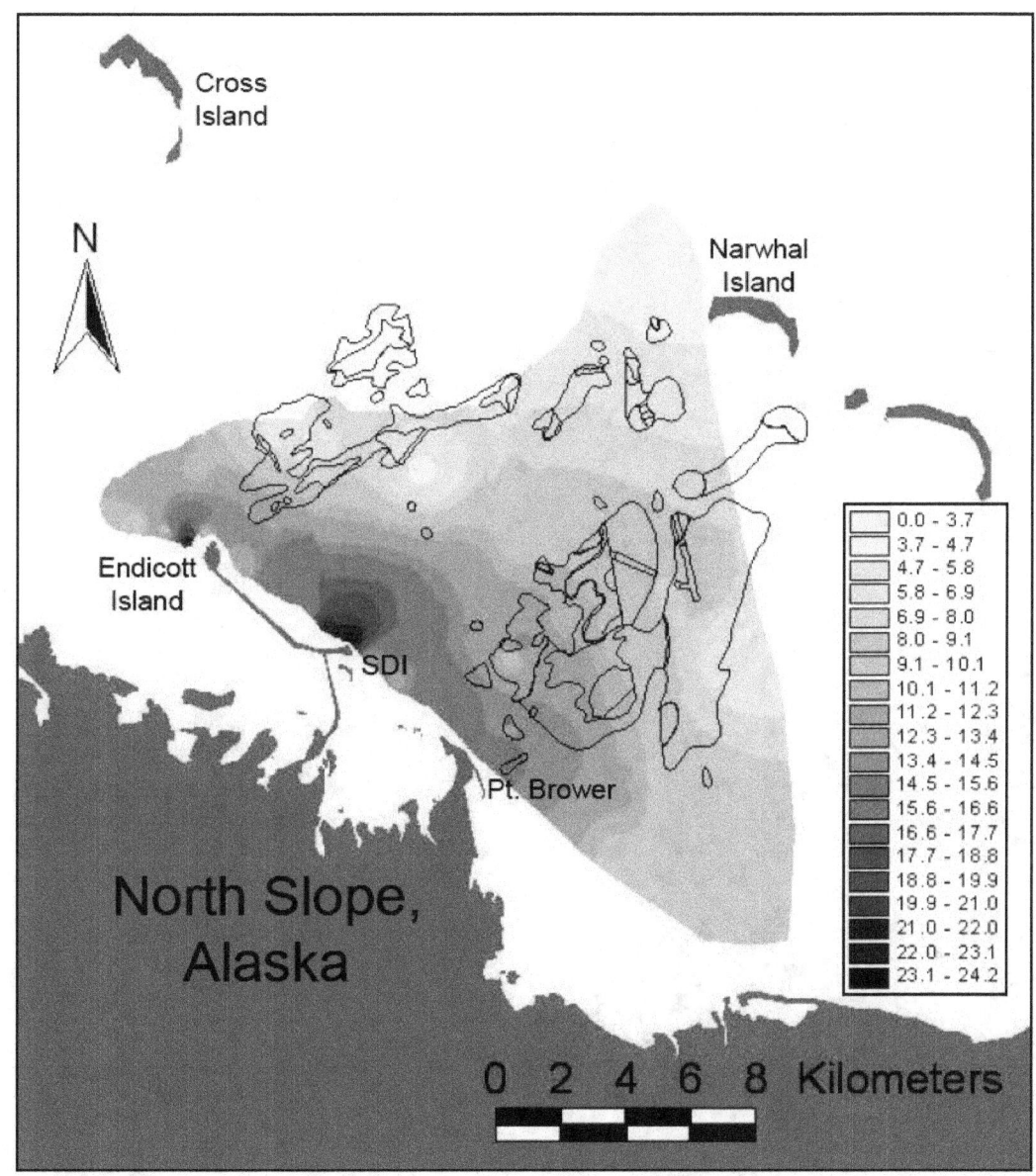

	0.0 - 3.7
	3.7 - 4.7
	4.7 - 5.8
	5.8 - 6.9
	6.9 - 8.0
	8.0 - 9.1
	9.1 - 10.1
	10.1 - 11.2
	11.2 - 12.3
	12.3 - 13.4
	13.4 - 14.5
	14.5 - 15.6
	15.6 - 16.6
	16.6 - 17.7
	17.7 - 18.8
	18.8 - 19.9
	19.9 - 21.0
	21.0 - 22.0
	22.0 - 23.1
	23.1 - 24.2

Figure 13. Interpolated TSS concentrations (mg L^{-1}) for summer 2001.   Areas of > 10% boulder cover are outlined in black.

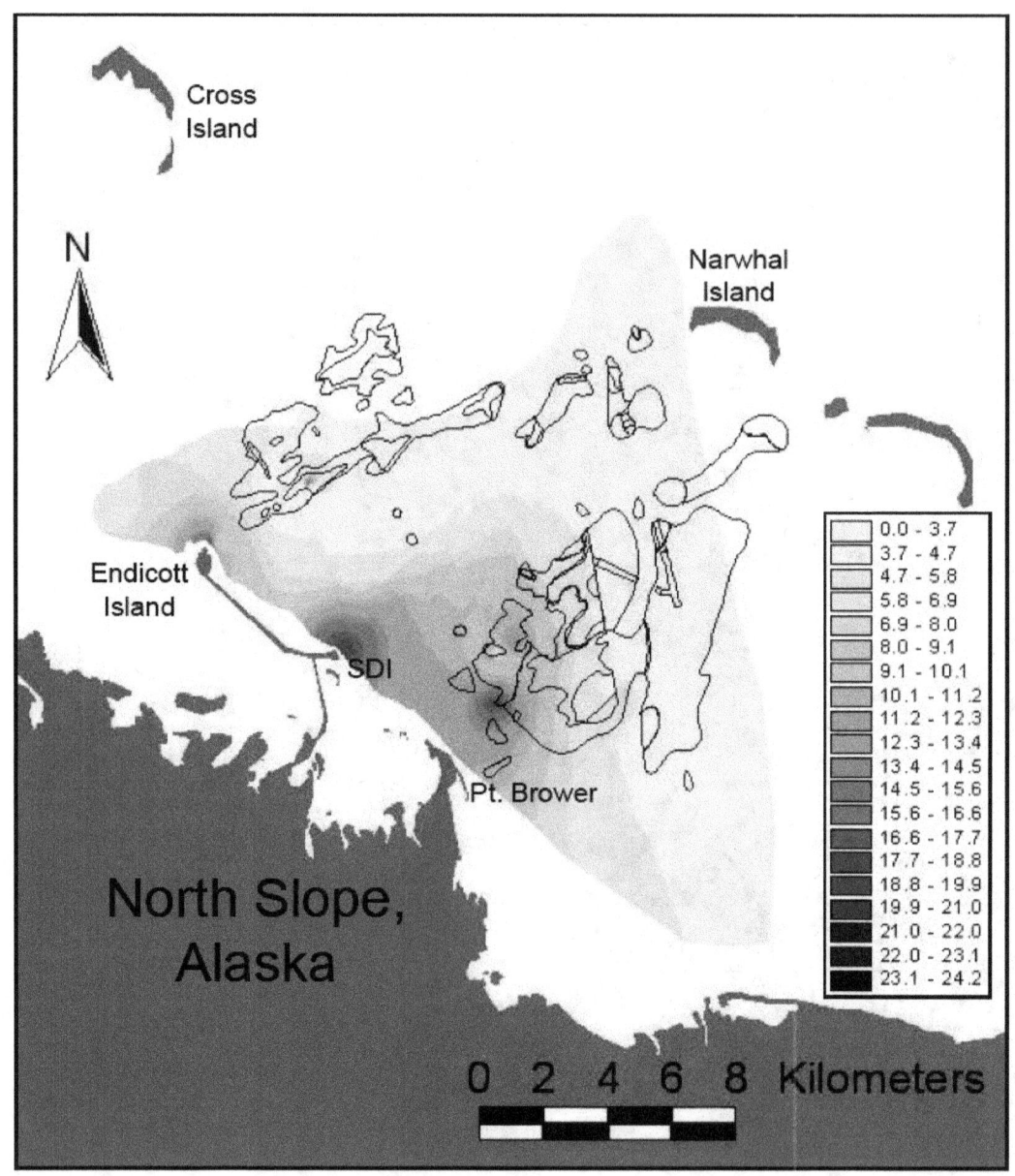

Figure 14. Interpolated TSS concentrations (mg L^{-1}) for summer 2002. Areas of > 10% boulder cover are outlined in black.

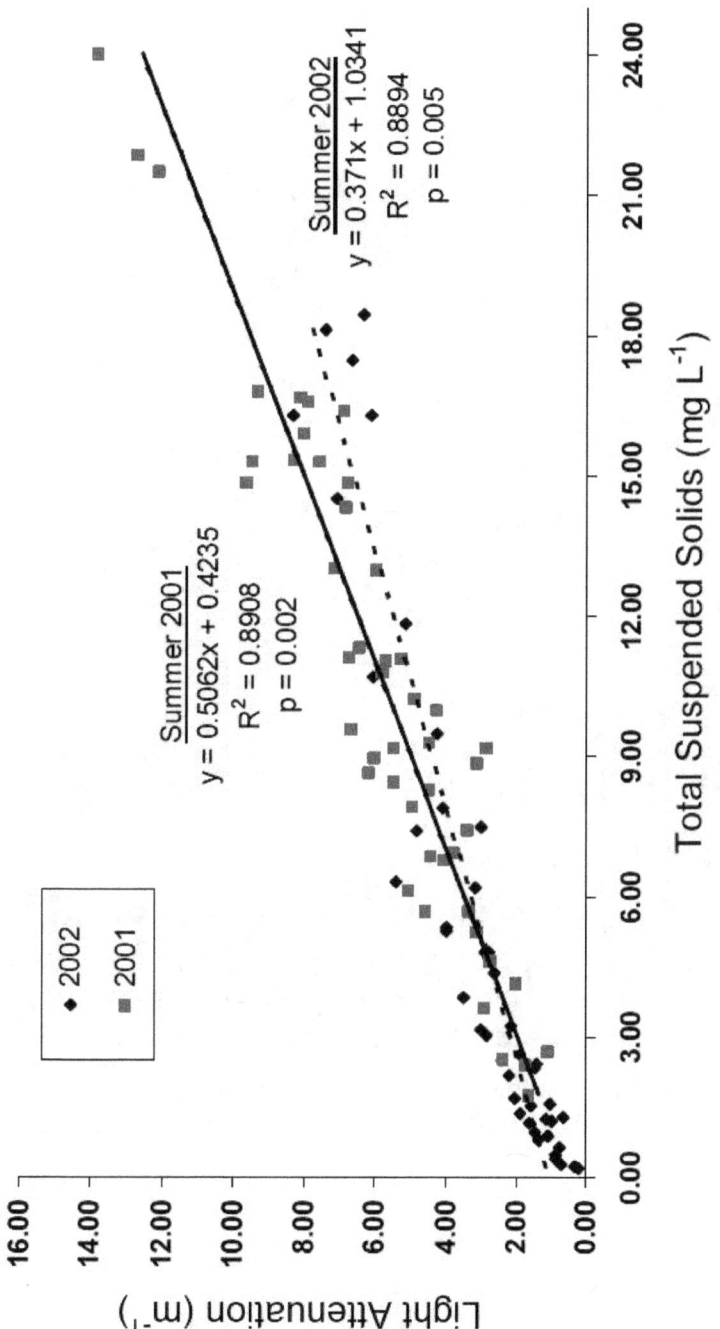

Figure 15. Correlations between light attenuation at 676 nm and TSS concentrations across Stefansson Sound in summers 2001 and 2002.

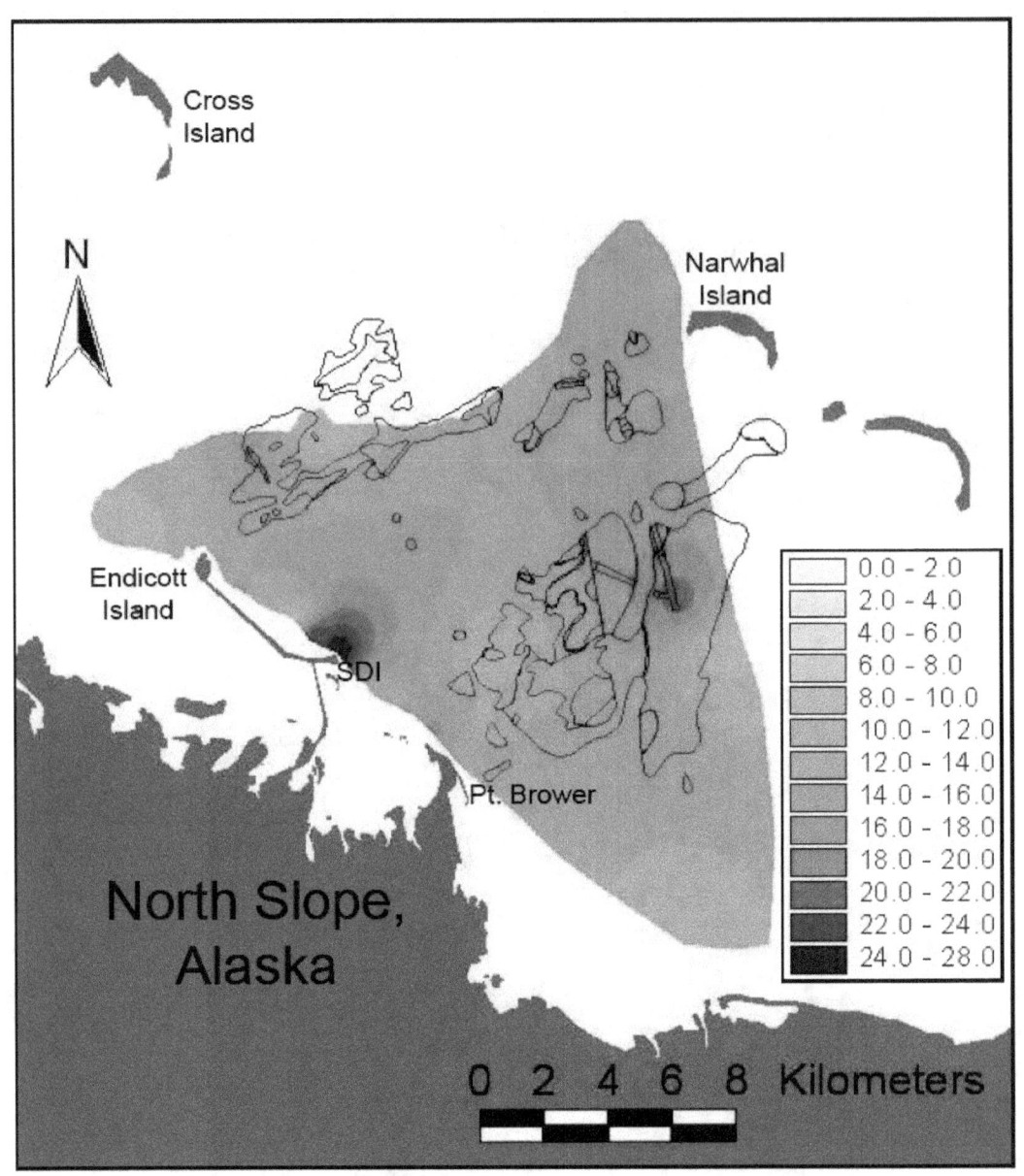

Figure 16. Chl *a* concentrations (μg L^{-1}) interpolated across Stefansson Sound during summer 2001. Areas of > 10% boulder cover are outlined in black.

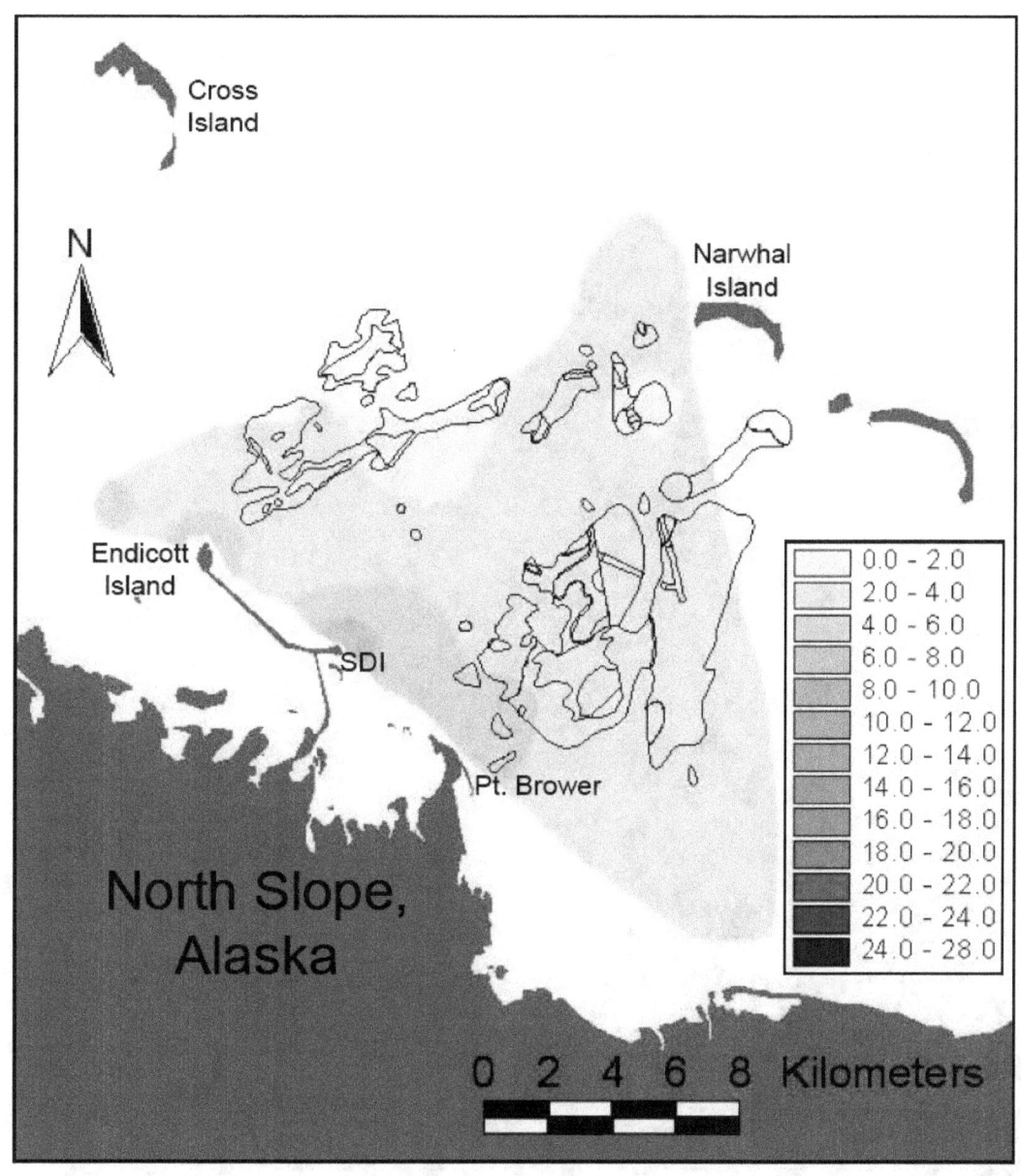

Figure 17. Chl *a* concentrations (μg L^{-1}) interpolated across Stefansson Sound during summer 2002. Areas of > 10% boulder cover are outlined in black.

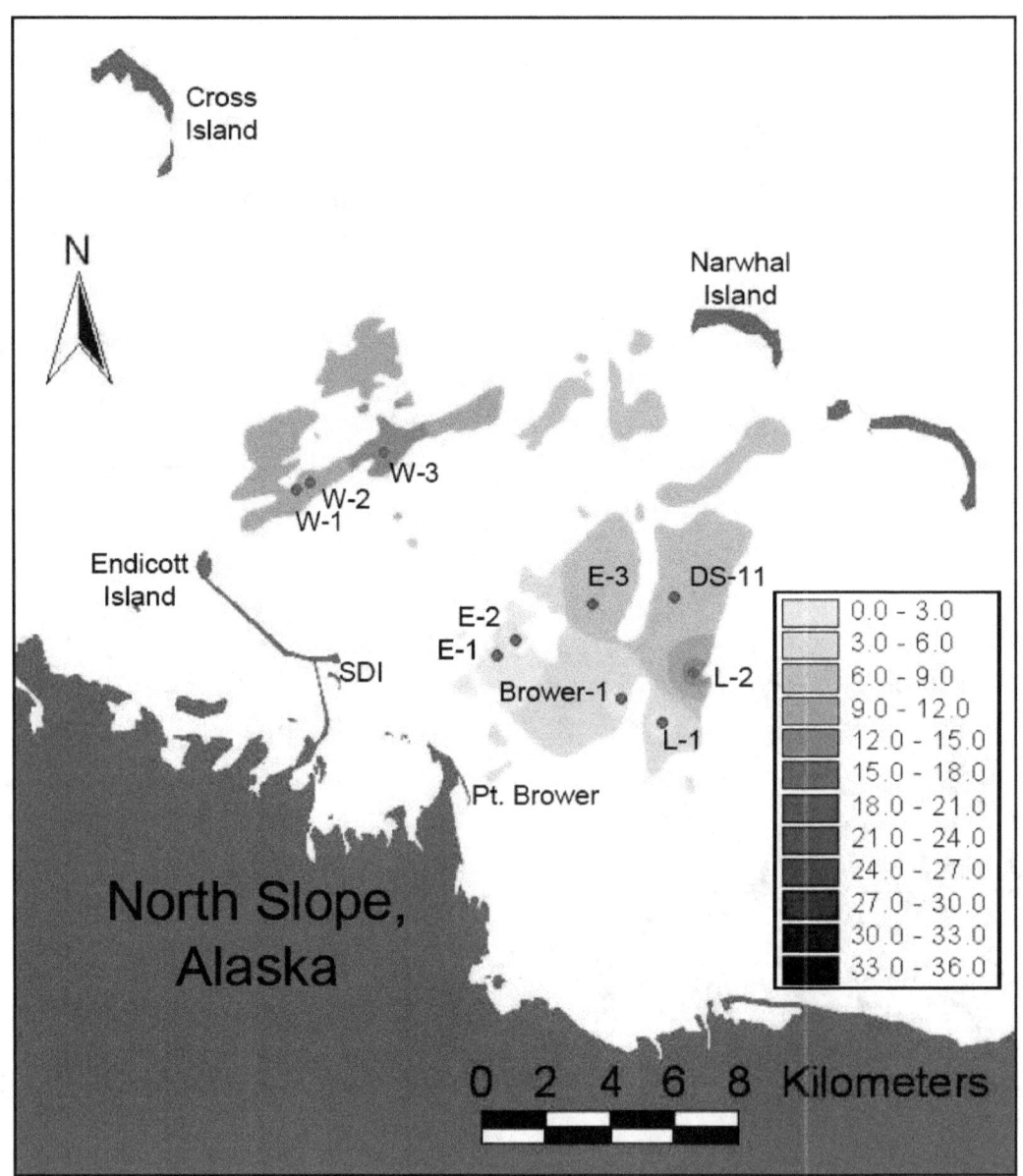

Figure 18. Interpolated production estimates (g C m^{-2} yr^{-1}) for a 60 day summer period within Stefansson Sound Boulder Patch for 2001 based on *in situ* measurements of TSS and IOPs. We assumed a biomass of 39.3 gdw m^{-2} for boulder cover 25% or greater and 10.0 gdw m^{-2} for boulder cover between 10-25% based on previous calculations (Dunton et al., 1982).

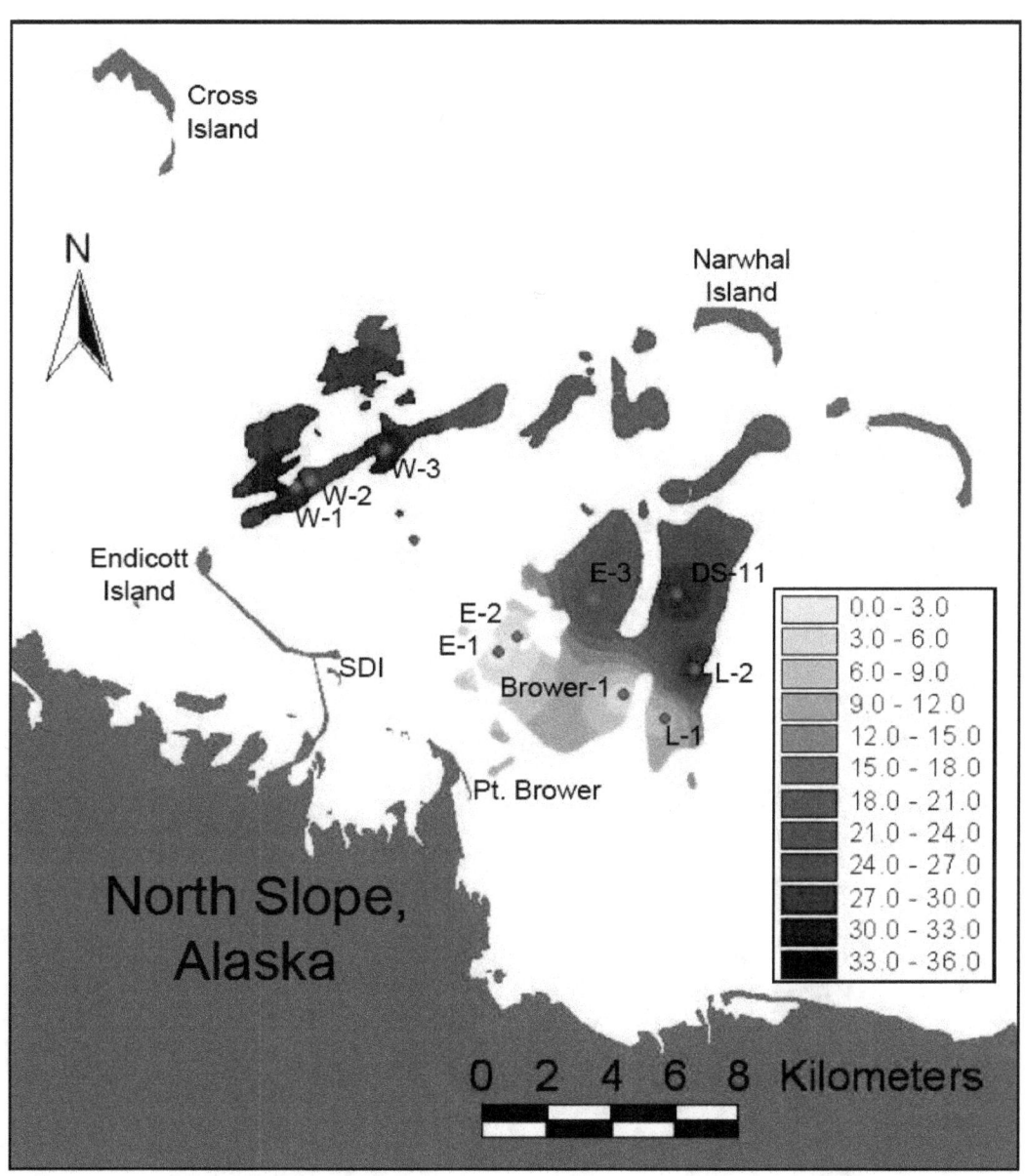

Figure 19. Interpolated production estimates ($g\ C\ m^{-2}\ yr^{-1}$) for a 60 day summer period within Stefansson Sound Boulder Patch for 2002 based on *in situ* measurements of TSS and IOPs. We assumed a biomass of 39.3 gdw m^{-2} for boulder cover 25% or greater and 10.0 gdw m^{-2} for boulder cover between 10-25% based on previous calculations (Dunton et al., 1982).

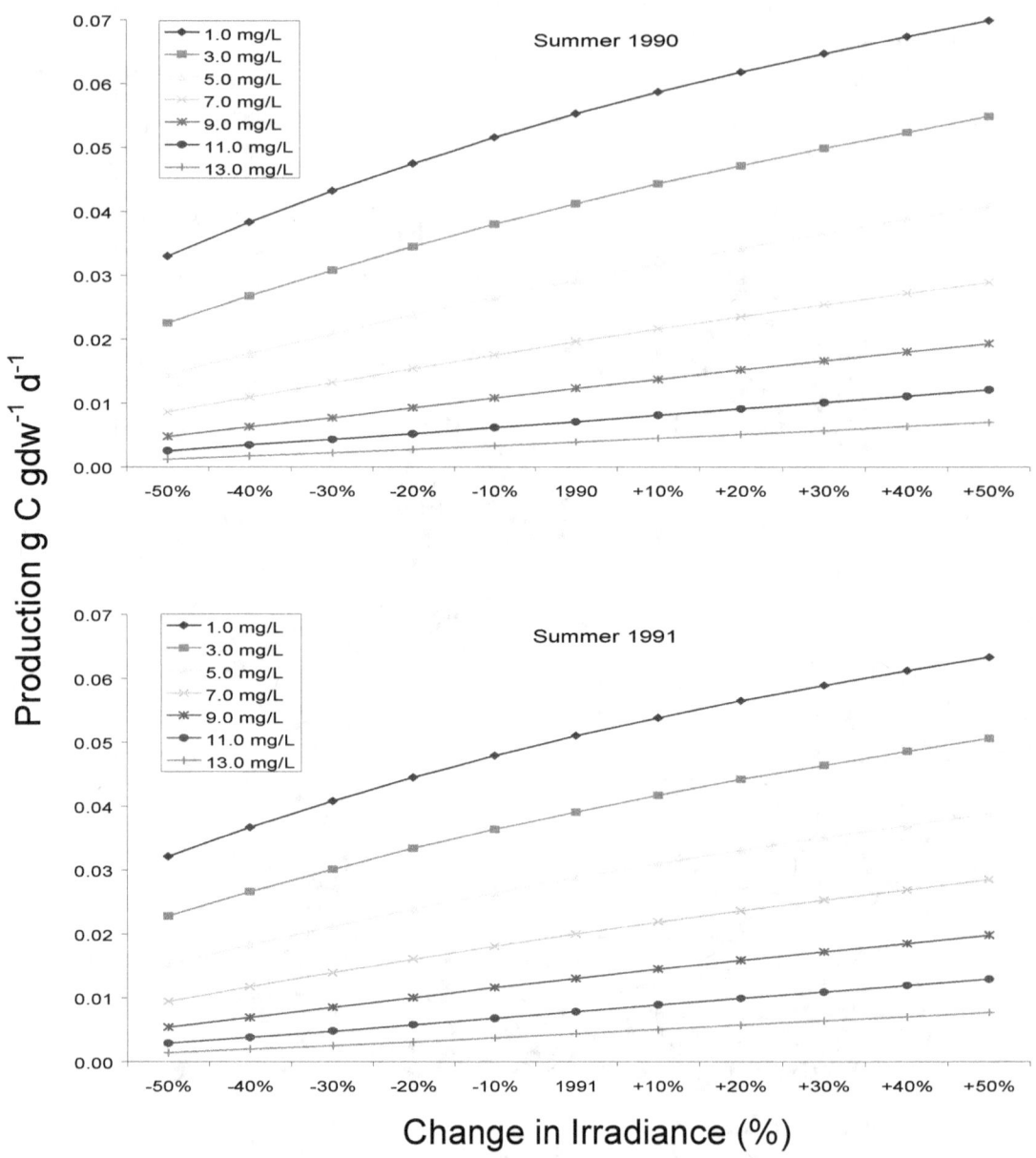

Figure 20. Estimated daily production as a function of percent summer surface irradiance based on hourly PAR measurements (μmols photons m^{-2} s^{-1}) collected in 1990 and 1991 by Dunton *et al*. (1992).

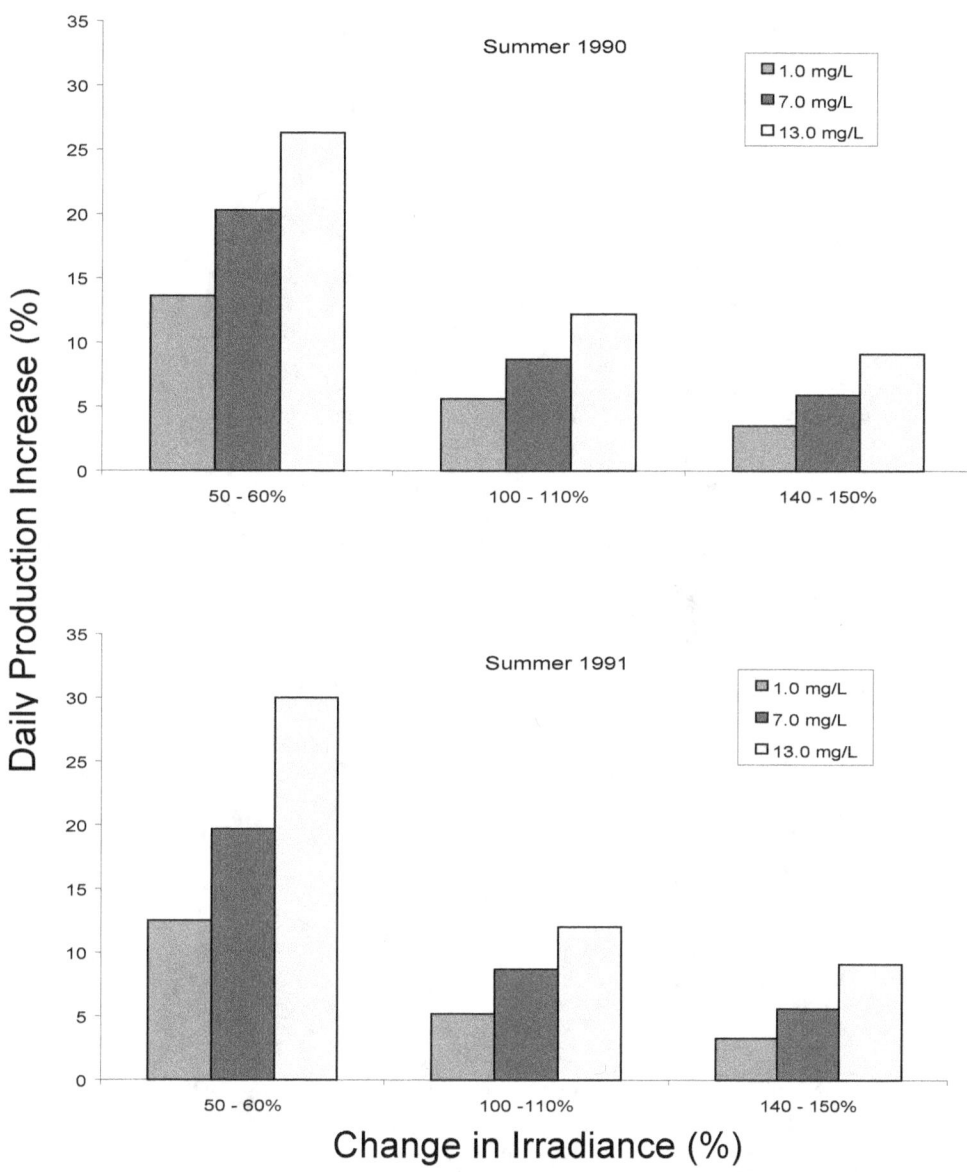

Figure 21. Percent increase in daily production as a function of modest (10%)
increases in summer irradiance under three different TSS levles (1,
7, and 13 mg L^{-1}). Modeled production estimates are based on
extremes in summer insolation derived from hourly surface PAR
(μmols photons m^{-2} s^{-1}) recorded in summers 1990 and 1991
(Dunton *et al.*, 1992).

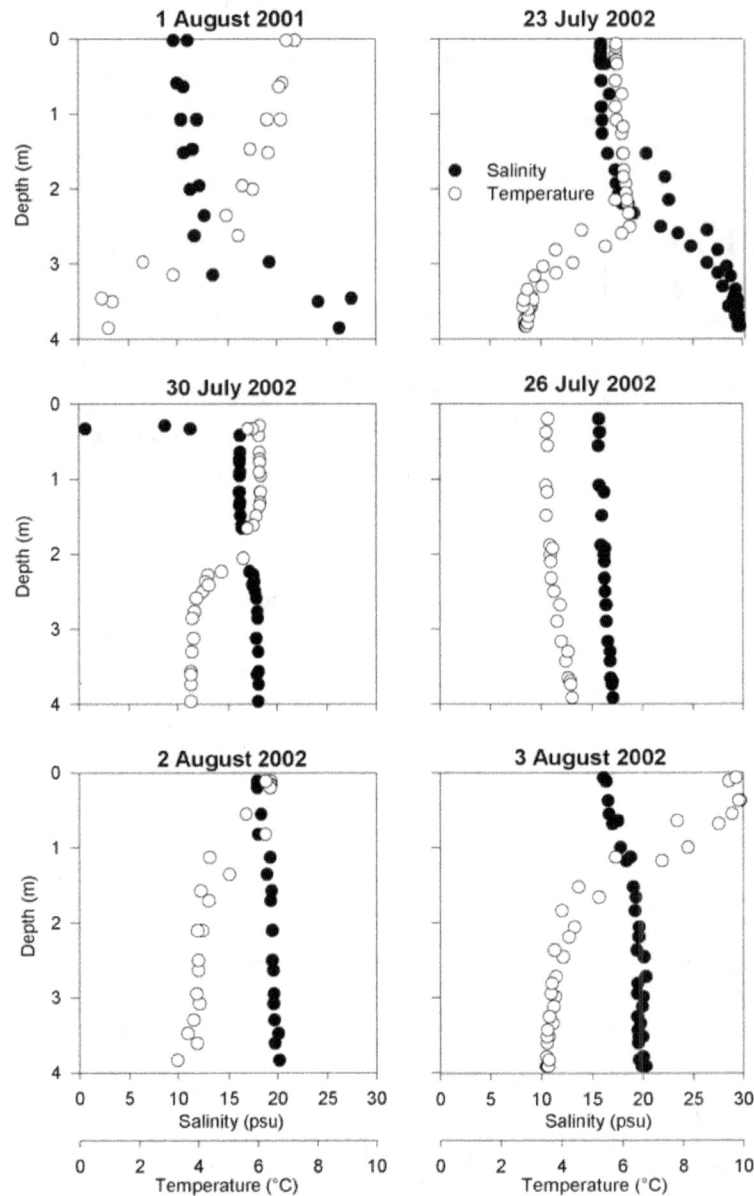

Figure 22. Vertical profiles of salinity and temperature at site E-1 in summers 2001 and 2002.

74

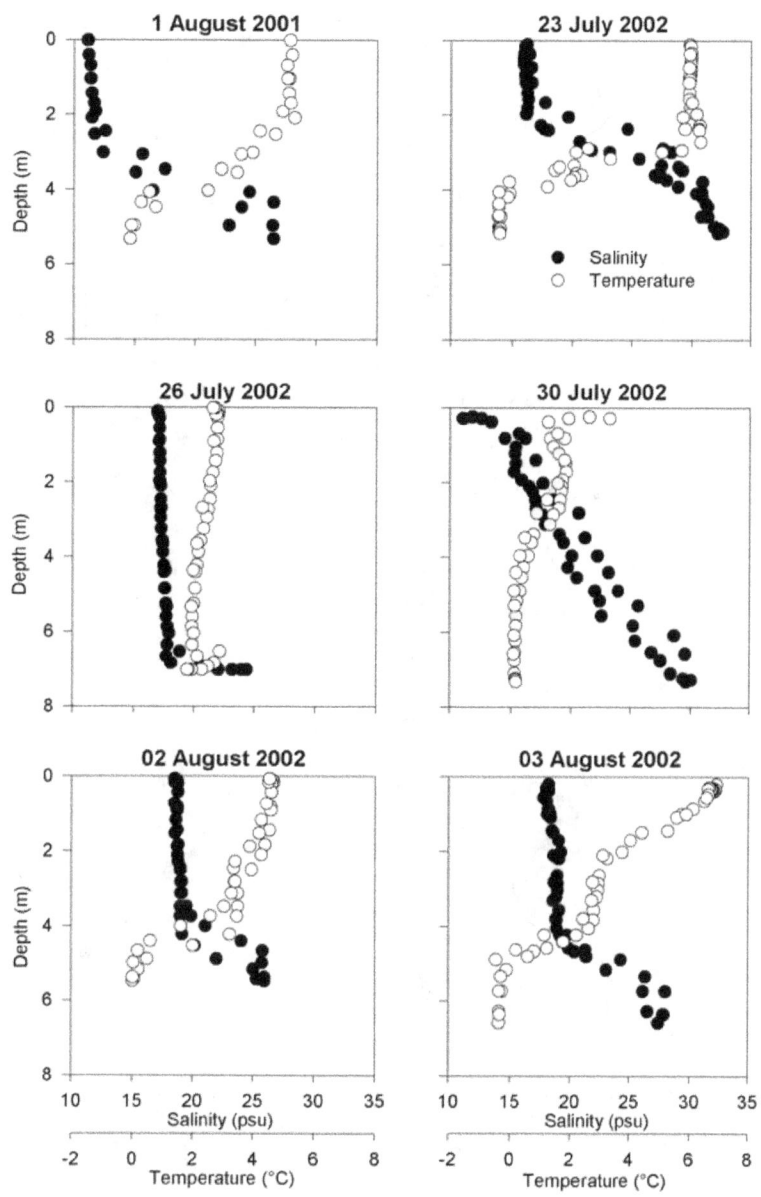

Figure 23. Vertical profiles of salinity and temperature at site
DS-11 in summers 2001 and 2002.

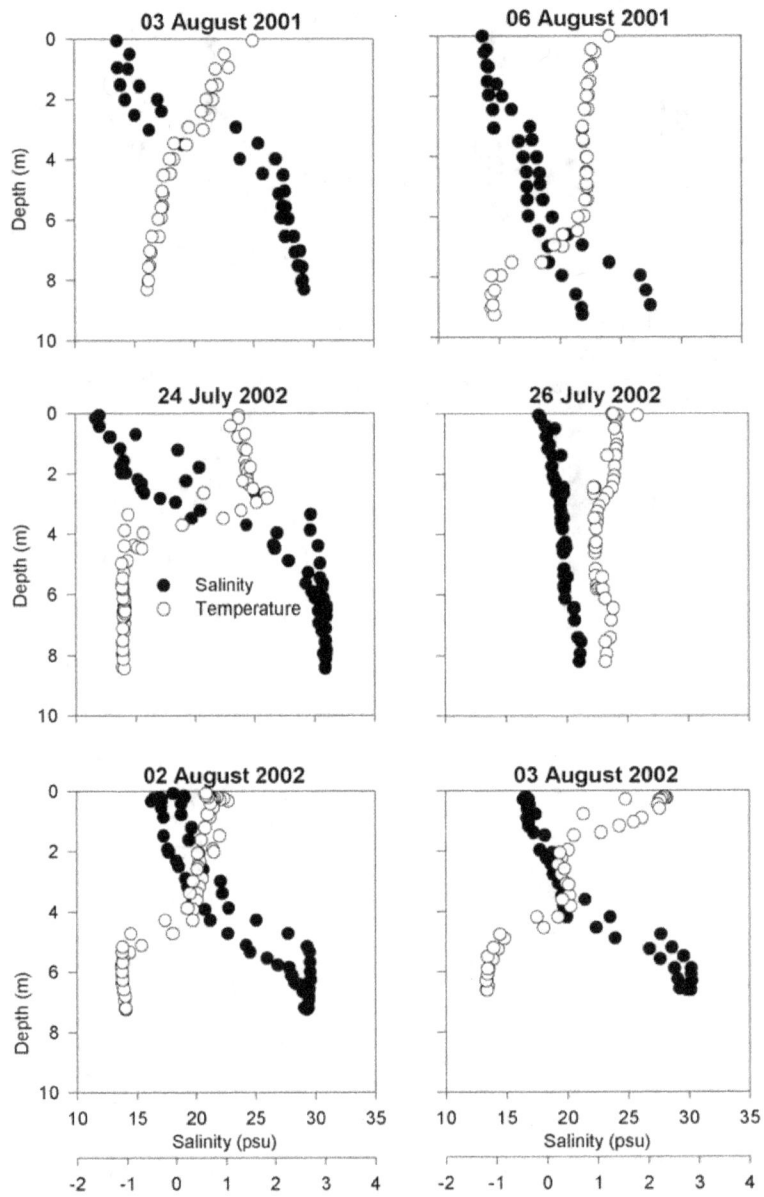

Figure 24. Vertical profiles of salinity and temperature at site
Narwhal Island in summers 2001 and 2002.

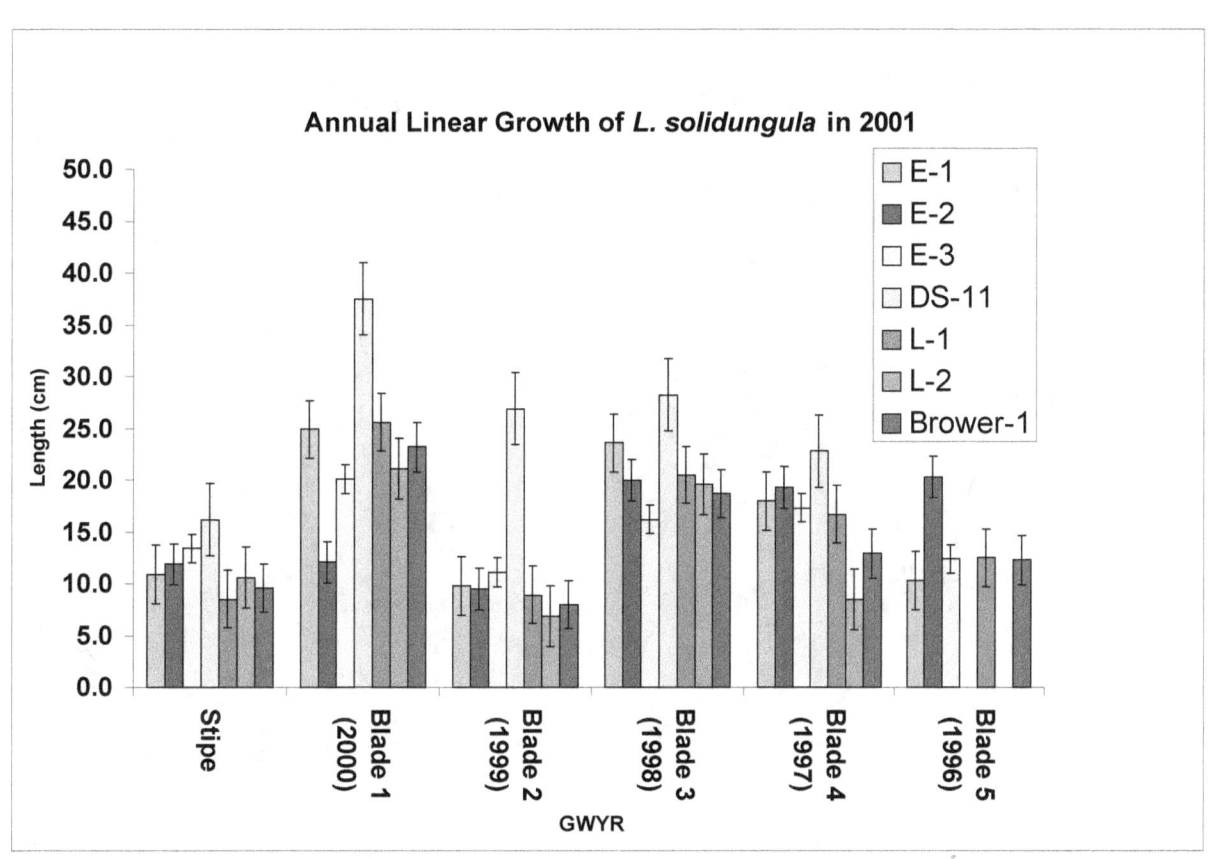

Figure 25. Annual linear growth of *Laminaria solidungula* blades at seven sites within Stefansson Sound Boulder Patch in summer 2001. Growth year (GWYR) for each blade is a defined period beginning 15 November one year and ending 15 November the following year. No specimens collected at DS-11 or L-2 possessed a 5th blade. Values are mean ± SE (n = 15 to 30).

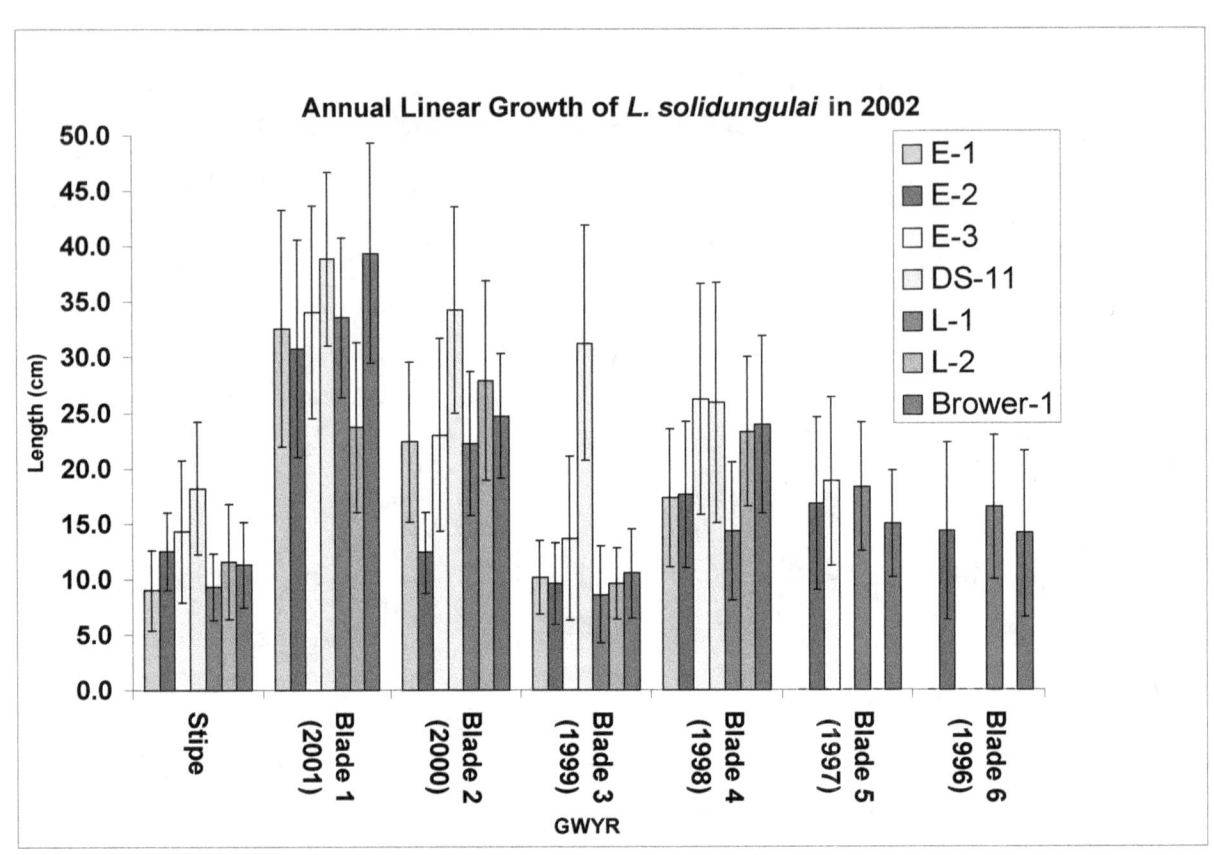

Figure 26. Annual linear growth of *Laminaria solidungula* blades at seven sites within Stefansson Sound Boulder Patch in 2002. Growth year (GWYR) for each blade is a defined period beginning 15 November one year and ending 15 November the following year. No specimens collected at E-1, DS-11 or L-2 possessed a 5th blade. Only sites E-2, L-1, and Brower-1 possessed a 6th blade. Values are mean ± SE (n = 15 to 30).

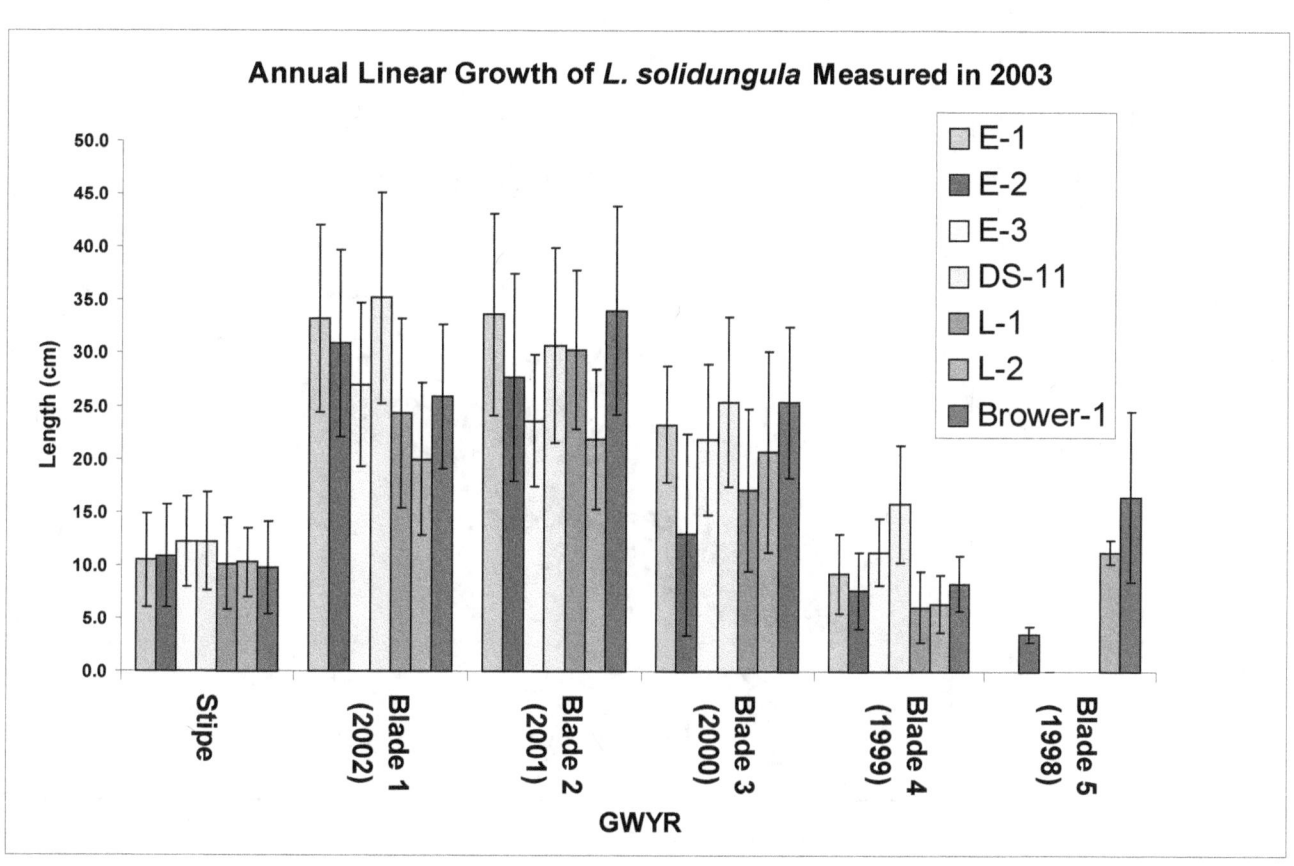

Figure 27. Annual linear growth of *Laminaria solidungula* blades at seven sites within the Stefansson Sound Boulder Patch measured in 2003. Growth year (GWYR) for each blade is a defined period beginning 15 November one year and ending 15 November the following year. No specimens collected at E-1, E-3, DS-11, or L-1 possessed a 5th blade. No specimens collected possessed a 6th blade. Values are mean ± SE (n = 15 to 30).

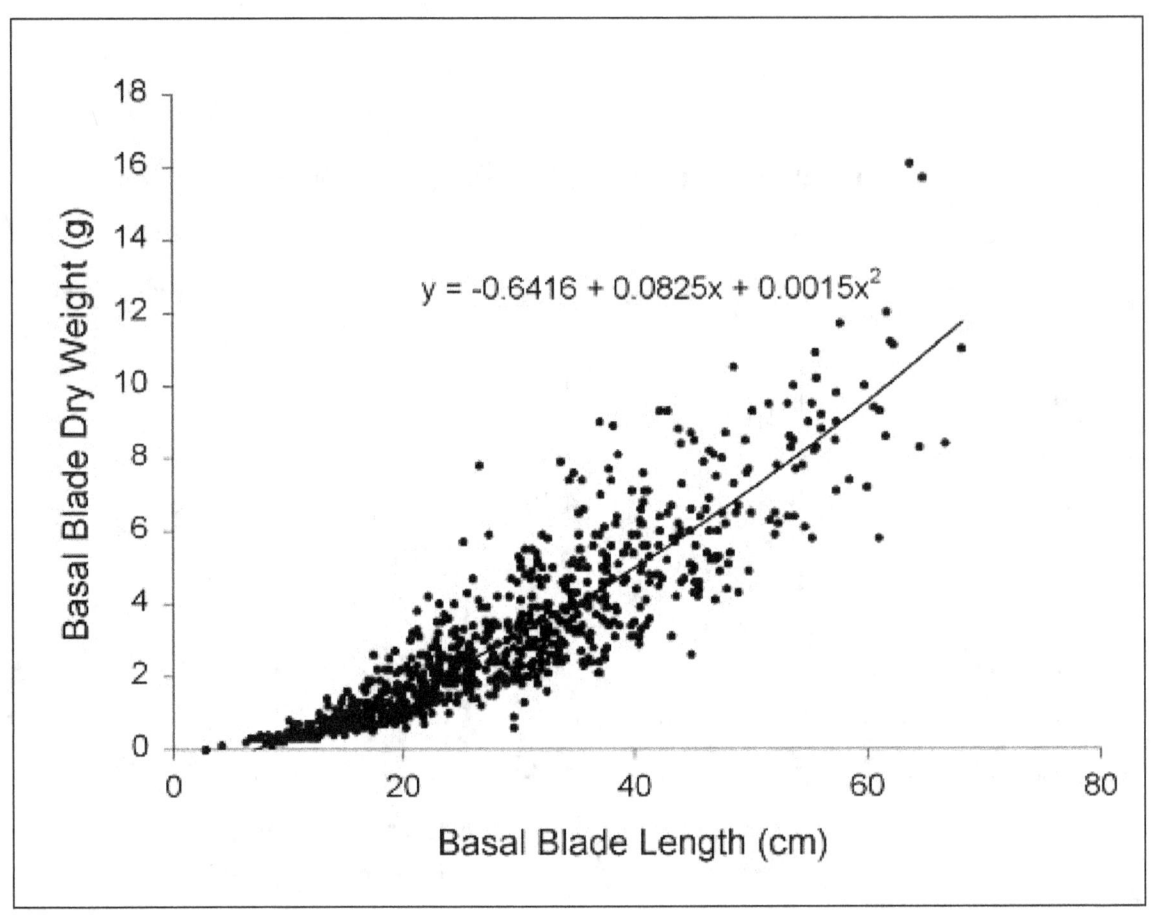

Figure 28. Correlation between basal blade dry weight (g) and basal blade length (cm) of *Laminaria solidungula* in Stefansson Sound Boulder Patch. Specimens were collected between 1980 – 1984 (n=820; Dunton *et al.*, 1982; Dunton and Schell, 1986).

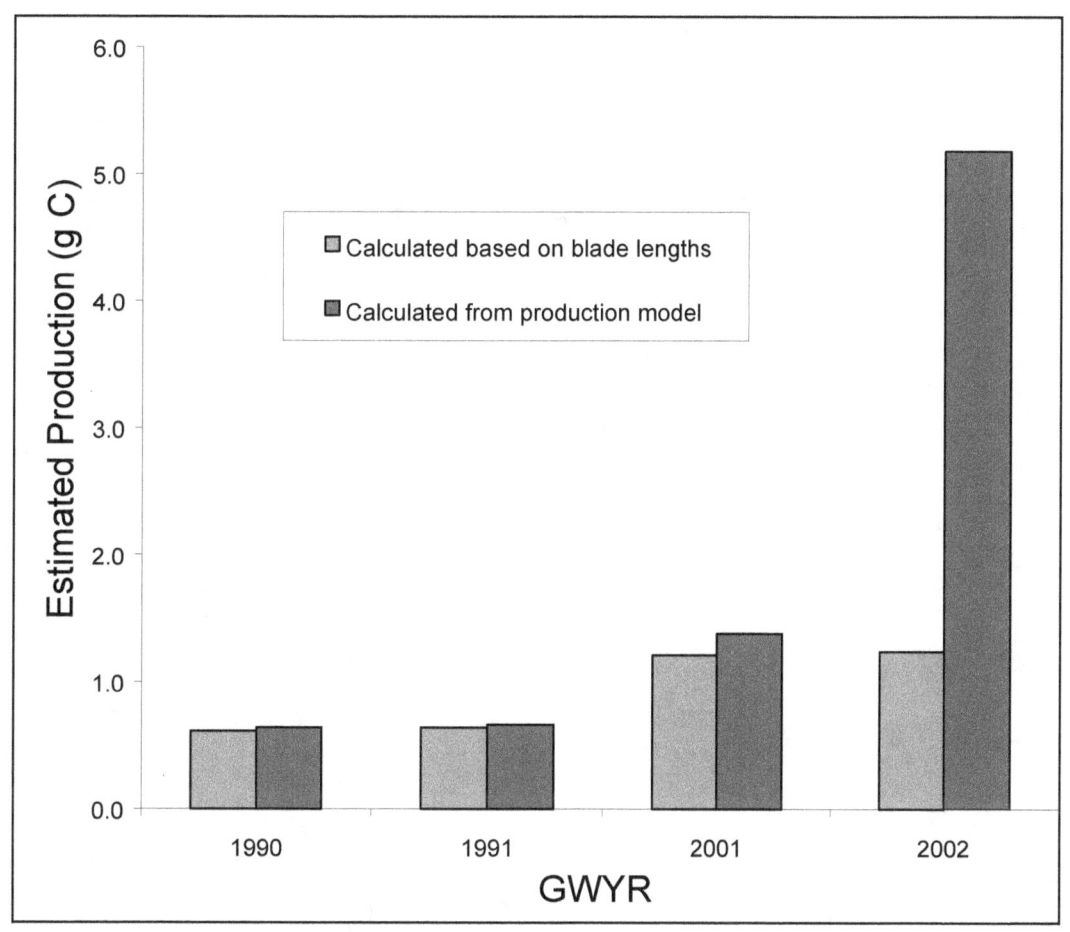

Figure 29. Comparison of actual production (g C) for an averaged sized kelp specimen at DS-11 based on basal blade lengths and model predictions over four different GWYRs.. Linear growth measurements were converted to carbon production based on analysis of published data (see Figure 28; Dunton and Schell, 1986). Production estimates for 1990 and 1991 used *in situ* measurements of modeled TSS from 2001 and measured values of irradiance collected in each respective year; surface light data from 1990 was used in model calculations for 2001 and 2002.

www.ingramcontent.com/pod-product-compliance
Lightning Source LLC
Chambersburg PA
CBHW081133290526
45795CB00006B/2225